FREEDOM'S ECHO

Angela Dorsey

FREEDOM'S ECHO

Original title: Freedom's Echo
Cover and inside illustrations: © 2008 Jennifer Bell
Cover layout: Stabenfeldt A/S

Typeset by Roberta L. Melzl
Editor: Bobbie Chase
Printed in Germany, 2008

ISBN: 978-1-934983-05-8

Stabenfeldt, Inc.
457 North Main Street
Danbury, CT 06811
www.pony4kids.com

Available exclusively through PONY.

HAILEY

Hailey stepped back as her best friend, Elaine, led Rain Shadow from his stall. When the monstrous black and white pinto sidestepped toward Hailey, her heart lunged against her chest and she lurched away.

"Be good, Rain," Elaine scolded, pulling him back to her side. Rain Shadow sighed, a resigned look in his brown eyes, and walked sedately behind her to the crossties, his massive hooves close to her heels.

How did Elaine do it? All the horse made Hailey want to do was run away, screaming.

"I can't believe you're canceling again," said Elaine, her attention back on Hailey. "And after I borrowed a horse for you and everything."

Hailey felt her ears turn red as the lie made its way to her lips. "I'm really sorry, Lainey. But it's not my fault." Thank goodness her long hair hid her ears. If Elaine knew she was lying to her, she'd never forgive her.

"Whose fault is it this time?" Elaine clipped the horse into the crossties and picked up a brush.

"Mom asked me to do some chores and…"

She stopped as Elaine turned toward her, her lips mere lines in her face.

Hailey stared at her in disbelief. "You think I'm lying to you?" she croaked. Finally, she'd been found out.

Elaine looked back at her horse. "No, I believe you," she said, looking cross. She ran the brush over the shiny black and white coat, her strokes confident as she groomed the muscular beast. "It just always seems so coincidental, that's all. You always have something else to do whenever I want you to come riding."

"Ready, Elaine?"

Hailey turned to see Jasmine striding toward them. Her boots gleamed and her short hair bounced as she walked. As usual, she looked perfect. A red horse walked briskly behind her, already saddled and bridled. Hailey pressed her back to the wall and her breath grew short as the red horse walked past.

"Just a couple minutes," said Elaine. She handed her brush to Hailey as she hurried toward the tack room. "Can you do his other side while I get the tack?"

Hailey looked down at the brush in her hand. "I… I'd love to, but I can't. I have to get going." She lobbed the brush toward the big bucket that held the rest of the grooming supplies – it was far too close to Rain Shadow – and miraculously, thankfully, it fell inside with a thunk.

"What's the matter, Hailey?" Jasmine taunted when Elaine was inside the tack room. "No, don't tell me. Let me guess. You have to rush off, right?"

Hailey thrust her chin in the air. "Some of us have people who rely on us, Jasmine."

"Now you sound just like my mom. Responsibility. Reliability. Integrity. Blah, blah, blah."

"No wonder you're failing English," Hailey retorted, narrowing her eyes.

"I'm not failing anything." All mocking was gone from Jasmine's voice. "And I'm not *afraid of horses* either."

"I'm not afraid."

Jasmine laughed. "The only one who doesn't know it

is Elaine because she refuses to believe you'd lie to her. But don't worry, I'll make sure she sees the truth."

Heat flooded Hailey's face. Was Jasmine threatening to take away her best friend?

Elaine's horse stamped its iron-shod hoof and Hailey automatically flung her arms up to protect herself.

Jasmine covered her smirk as Elaine came out of the tack room, carrying a western saddle with Rain Shadow's bridle draped over the saddle horn.

"I'll call you tonight, Lainey," said Hailey, hating that her voice trembled. Jasmine was so much more beastly than the horses.

"Are you sure you can't come? It's going to be so much fun," Elaine said as she lifted the saddle high onto the black and white back. The horse shifted forward in an effort to avoid the cinch.

Hailey stepped back as calmly as she could. "Wish I could. Sorry."

"You always miss out, Hailey," Jasmine said in a falsely sweet voice. "We can go riding tomorrow too. You can ask your mom tonight, to make sure it's okay, and we can all ride to the lake and go swimming."

"That sounds great, Jasmine," Elaine said, enthusiastically. She moved to Rain Shadow's head and slipped the metal bar into his mouth, the leather over his ears.

"Yeah. *Great*," said Hailey.

"Don't sound so excited," said Jasmine. She gathered her reins and climbed into the red horse's saddle.

"It'll be nice to go swimming," said Hailey, ignoring Jasmine's sarcastic comment. At least this time she was telling the truth.

Jasmine turned her horse toward Hailey and asked

him to walk. They were coming so close… the horse was going to step on her… she couldn't breathe…

Hailey couldn't help herself; her feet had a will of their own as they carried her down the barn aisle. Hoofbeats clattered behind her and Hailey broke into a jog. The hoof beats started to trot. A light sweat burst from her forehead. Hailey ran faster, but still they came closer, closer.

"Wait for me!" Elaine called.

The hoofbeats stopped.

Hailey ran through the doorway and moved to the side, pressing her back against the open door. Her heart was beating a hundred miles an hour and she couldn't catch her breath. How close had they come? Would Jasmine and her horse have run right over her if Elaine hadn't yelled to wait?

Only one thing she knew for sure: this was a preview of tomorrow if she couldn't get out of the ride to the lake. Jasmine would expose her, plus embarrass and humiliate her as much as possible. And she would hurt and embarrass Elaine too, making her feel stupid and betrayed for believing Hailey's lie for so long.

Jasmine's horse strutted out of the barn, his rider looking even haughtier than he did. Hailey tried to slink out of sight, but it was too late. Jasmine locked eyes with her, a small smile touching her face. Then Elaine was riding Rain Shadow out of the barn.

Elaine pulled her horse to a stop. "It's just no fair. You always have chores to do."

"I know. Sorry."

Jasmine kicked her horse into a trot, but Elaine held Rain Shadow back. The massive creature bobbed his head, impatient, and struck the ground with his front hoof. Hailey could barely stop herself from shrinking back.

"But tomorrow we can go, like Jasmine said," said Elaine. "It'll be fun."

"Sure." Hailey's voice was barely a croak. "If Mom and Dad let me."

"We'll ask your mom tonight, after the play, okay?" said Elaine.

"Okay," Hailey said, feeling miserable.

"Great. See you then." Elaine asked Rain Shadow to walk. "Don't worry, your mom will say yes," she yelled back over her shoulder. "Once she knows how much you want to go."

Hailey waved to Elaine, but her friend didn't see her. She was already intent on catching up to Jasmine.

Hailey crossed her arms over her stomach to wait until the butterflies settled. What was she going to do now? What chance did she have of keeping her terrible secret? None, absolutely none.

"Are you okay?"

Hailey spun around. Penny Martin, a girl two grades ahead of her in school, was standing beside her with a concerned look on her face. She kept a horse at this stable, too.

"I'm okay," said Hailey.

"You look so pale," said Penny. She glanced back at the driveway as if she was expecting someone, then turned back to Hailey. "Are you sure you're okay?"

"I'm fine," Hailey gasped and hurried away from the older girl, her head down. Everyone else seemed to notice the fear that consumed her when she was around horses – and tomorrow Elaine would too. If only she hadn't lied that first day. If only she'd told her friend how she felt.

It wasn't as if she *wanted* to be afraid of horses. In fact, she always thought she'd love them. They were so beautiful in pictures and on TV. But when Elaine started taking riding lessons at Evergreen Stables and Hailey met her first horse face to face, she couldn't stop shaking. The horse was just so big, so dangerous looking. It could squish her with one movement if it wanted. Thankfully Elaine had been so excited she hadn't noticed Hailey's terror – and after that, Hailey lied.

She sighed as she turned onto the quiet country road. A long, boring afternoon stretched ahead of her, with nothing to do but think about what a horrible person she was, lying to her best friend. If she'd been honest with Elaine to begin with, her friend would've helped her to get over her fear. Hailey grimaced. That was exactly the reason she hadn't told Elaine – the idea of walking up to Rain Shadow, of getting within range of those big hooves, those yellow teeth, those amazingly fast front legs…

A whinny floated toward her on the warm summer breeze and Hailey stopped short, then inhaled sharply when two horses strode around the corner: a red and white spotted adult horse and a black baby horse with a white mark on its chest. And the baby's eyes… there was something unusual about them. They didn't blend into the darkness of its face. Were they *blue*?

They were. How pretty! A bubbliness touched Hailey's heart. She'd found a horse pretty again. Maybe there was hope for her yet.

The foal stopped, forcing the mare to stop behind her, and raised its lovely sculpted head to neigh a greeting. Hailey's delight changed instantly to terror. She couldn't see a rope on the young horse. Her gaze darted to the girl riding the mare. Surely she wouldn't let it run loose, even on this empty road.

The foal stepped toward her and automatically Hailey shrank away.

Then she noticed the sheen of a black leather halter on the fine head. A dark rope led back to the mare. What a relief! The foal reached the end of its tether and stopped.

"Hi," the girl said.

Hailey focused on her face. Jani Preston, Penny's best friend. They must be meeting at the stables to go for a ride together. "Hi."

"You don't need to worry. I have a rope on her."

Hailey blushed. "I'm not afraid," she said. Attempting to prove her words, she somehow forced her trembling legs to carry her toward the two horses. As long as she didn't get too close, she should be okay. And at least one of these horses was small. The big one wasn't as huge or energetic as Rain Shadow either, and if both horses stayed calm until after she'd gotten past them, everything would be okay. Surely she could do that much.

FREEDOM

Freedom snorted and stopped short, her blue eyes locked on the girl. She'd seen a number of humans in her short life, but none like this one. This one was different, though she wasn't sure why. It was as if there was an invisible shiver in the air around her.

The dark filly glanced back at her human. Did Jani see the difference? She didn't think so. Her girl didn't seem surprised or intrigued by this child.

Freedom looked back at the younger girl again and neighed – *Who are you?* Maybe she'd understand and answer. Maybe that was what was special about her.

When she only shrank from the sound, Freedom shook her head and snorted. So the girl couldn't communicate with her. That wasn't different at all.

If she could just get closer maybe she could smell the difference… Jani stopped her with a light tug on the lead rope. "She's afraid, Freedom. Don't you see?" Freedom did see, but Jani must know that she wouldn't hurt the girl. She only wanted to discover her specialness. She only wanted to understand what was so extraordinary about this ordinary looking girl.

Jani and the girl started talking, but Freedom didn't bother listening. There was nothing to learn from the humans' speech. She craned her head to the side to watch the girl from a different angle, then lowered her head. From every direction, she looked the same – long, chestnut hair bright in the sun, eyes a clear forever blue, and freckles across her cheeks.

The filly snorted and leaned forward, inhaled. She really needed to smell the girl, or better yet, touch her. It was important that she discover what was so unusual about this girl, because if she was the only one who sensed this indefinable thing, then what made this girl different had to be a message for her.

But what could that message be?

JANI

"You see? She likes you. She wants to meet you," Jani said to the younger girl.

Hailey took another step forward. "Are… are you sure she can't get loose?"

"She wouldn't hurt you even if she was. I promise," Jani answered.

Hailey paused and studied Freedom. "She's pretty. I love her eyes."

Freedom bobbed her head; Hailey edged back.

"She just wants you to pet her."

"I can't, I mean, I'm in a hurry," Hailey said and started to walk a wide berth around Jani, Keeta, and Freedom.

"I was afraid of horses too at first," said Jani, though it was an exaggeration. She'd been mildly cautious, while Hailey looked completely terrified.

Hailey stopped. "I'm not…" Her voice faded as she stared at the black filly.

"Then why don't you pet her?"

Hailey looked up at Jani with desperate eyes. "You were afraid? Really?"

"At first, but not anymore. Keeta's my best friend now." She stroked the red and white mare on the shoulder. "There's nothing to worry about with Freedom. She's gentle and she seems to like you. I've never seen her act so interested in anyone before."

"Really?"

Jani smiled and nodded. "Really."

Hailey squeezed her eyes shut for a moment, then looked up at Jani. "If I tell you something, do you promise not to say anything? To anyone?"

"Sure."

"Say you promise."

"I promise."

Hailey breathed deeply. "You're right. I'm afraid of horses. I don't want to be, but I am."

Jani smiled. "It's kind of obvious. Sorry."

"My best friend doesn't know yet. More than anything, I want to get used to them, so that she never finds out." Hailey looked down at the ground.

"Freedom's smaller than other horses. Why don't you move closer to her and see what happens?"

Hailey stared at the foal as if she were a three headed monster, then held out her hand – possibly more to stop the filly from attacking than to let her sniff her hand.

"You can do it," Jani encouraged.

Hailey took a step toward the filly.

Jani let out the lead rope a little as Freedom leaned toward Hailey. Her muzzle was just inches from the younger girl's hand when she inhaled – and scrambled back, her eyes wild.

Hailey cried out and jumped backwards.

Jani tightened her hold on the lead rope. Why would Freedom startle like that? Hailey looked perfectly harmless. "Sorry about that," she said. "Foals are unpredictable sometimes. I should've warned you. You did really great though. Want to try again?"

When Hailey didn't answer, Jani slid from Keeta's back and turned the mare to face the younger girl. "Come up to Keeta. She's gentle *and* well trained."

"She's too big. I'd still rather try the little one."

Jani pulled on Freedom's lead rope, bringing the foal to her side. "I'll hold her. Just remember to take your time and let her smell you first."

Hailey drew a deep breath. "Okay." But her feet didn't move.

"You can do it," Jani said.

Hailey took another deep breath. Her face was as white as a summer cloud and the fingers she held out were shaking. She closed her eyes and lifted one foot – then put it back down.

"You know, my dad told me once that there's only one way to be brave and that's to face something you fear," Jani said. "If you aren't afraid of something, you're not really being brave when you face it."

Hailey's round eyes met Jani's. "I can't," she whispered. "I just can't do it."

Freedom nickered gently and leaned slightly forward.

"See? She's saying she's sorry. She didn't mean to scare you like that."

"I can't." This time Hailey's voice was more definite.

"That's okay," Jani said, turning back to Keeta. "You shouldn't feel too bad. You got close to her once. That's something." She climbed into the saddle. When she looked back at Hailey, the girl had retreated a number of steps. Tears were shining on her cheeks.

"It's going to take time, Hailey. That's all. Don't cry." Jani felt her own eyes prickle with tears as she looked at the girl's miserable face. "Come over to my house tomorrow. If you have a fence between you and them, you might feel safer."

"Really?"

"Sure."

Hailey nodded. "Okay, I'll come over tomorrow. Thanks, Jani."

"Anytime." A drop of rain plopped on Jani's arm and she looked up. The sun was disappearing behind a dark cloud. "Ew, rain. Again."

"I better go."

"Me too. Penny's waiting."

Jani asked her mare to walk on, but pulled her to a stop when Hailey called her name.

"You still won't tell anyone will you?"

"No. I promised."

A shadow of a smile touched Hailey's face. "Thanks," she said again, and turned away. Jani watched her hurry away along the country road. Poor Hailey. She couldn't even imagine how awful it would be to be so deathly afraid of something – especially horses!

She sighed and nudged Keeta into a walk again. The mare stepped out eagerly. Moments later, the sprinkle turned into a downpour. Keeta tugged on the reins and Jani let her lope. She turned the mare into the Evergreen Stables driveway.

Penny and Sunny, her palomino gelding, looked out from the big barn doors, distasteful expressions on both of their faces. Obviously, there would be no more riding today – just enough for Jani to get Keeta and Freedom home as soon as the downpour lessened. After three days of rain, it was enough to make anyone depressed.

FREEDOM

As soon as they were in their stall, Freedom cuddled up next to her dam. The warm barn quickly evaporated their dampness and steam lifted into the air. The sounds of Keeta rhythmically chewing her grain filled the space with comfort. Freedom sighed. She was tired. It had been a fun day; first the ride over to Sunny's barn and meeting the strange girl, then introducing herself to all the horses in the stables while Jani and Penny waited for the rain to stop. It hadn't stopped, and so the ride home had been especially fun, with lots of puddles for splashing.

She ate a few mouthfuls of her dam's grain, then meandered to the corner and folded her legs to lie down. Keeta looked back at her and nickered. Settled in the straw, Freedom whinnied softly in return. Her head drooped.

Only one thing bothered her about the day: that she couldn't name what was so different about the girl she'd met. She closed her eyes, imagined the shiver of air around the child. Was it caused by her disease? Freedom had noted her illness the moment she'd laid eyes on her.

And sniffing the girl's hand had been a surprise when the freezing cold entered her nostrils. Maybe something was going to happen to the girl that was going to make her very cold?

Most mysterious of all was that she seemed to be the only one who recognized anything different about the girl. Not even Keeta had noted her uniqueness.

Was it only her imagination?

Freedom snorted softly. No, it was something real, something even ominous, as if the girl was in danger, as if she needed …

That was it! Something in the girl was calling for help, and she, Freedom, was the only one who could hear.

The filly scrambled to her hooves, all thoughts of rest gone from her mind as she started to pace.

Help with what? The girl's unreasonable fear? Her disease? Or were these elements of a much bigger problem?

She had to discover the truth soon, for it stood to reason: if she was the only one who could hear this child, she was also the only one who could save her.

JANI

"Bravo! Bravo!" Jani cheered with the rest of the crowd as they all stood to applaud the actors. Her voice was almost completely engulfed by her dad's enthusiastic shouts, as he yelled the same beside her. On the edge of the stage, Jani's mom took a final bow along with the rest of the cast, her face lit up with a wide smile. Then the curtain was down.

"That was awesome!"

"Your mom's a star."

"I never knew how cool she was, I mean, *is*, before."

"I know. She's much too good for the likes of your old dad."

"You're cool too, Dad. Kind of. In a way." Jani giggled, then ducked when he tried to ruffle her hair. She was getting much too old for that sort of thing.

The lights came on and people starting moving toward the exits. Jani looked around for some of her friends from school, but didn't see anyone. She and her dad wouldn't be going anywhere for a while, not until her mom was ready to go. "All the other actors were good too," she said, sitting down again.

Her dad sat down beside her.

"But you know what the neatest thing was?" Jani continued. "They looked like they were having fun."

"You should think about auditioning for the next play, Jani. You'd be great out there." He glanced sideways at her.

"I couldn't."

"Why not?"

Jani wished she hadn't said a word. "I just don't think I'd be very good, that's all."

"Chicken." He said it quietly, but that seemed to make the word even more irritating. "Bock, bock, bock."

"Dad!" Jani slugged him in the shoulder.

"Ouch, I think you broke my ribs," he groaned and clutched his opposite shoulder, then he jumped up. Jani's mom was walking toward them, her step light and her face glowing.

"The star of the show! Anna, you were wonderful!" He pulled his wife into a hug.

"You were, Mom. Really," said Jani, when the two separated.

"Aw, you guys are my family. You *have* to say that."

"Yeah, but we really mean it this time," said Jani, then realized how that sounded. "I mean, you really were awesome. I mean, *are* awesome."

Her mom laughed. "Thanks, honey." She put her hand on Jani's shoulder.

"Jani was just telling me that she wants to join the theater guild."

"Really? Oh, that would be fabulous. Hey, I know. You should come backstage while I finish getting ready to go. I'll introduce you to our director. Maybe in our next play we'll need a child actor."

"Or a very short person," said Jani's dad.

"Or a sneaky one," said Jani. "You'd be perfect for that role, Dad."

"Ah, but you must understand, I knew you wanted me to say something," he said and tugged on a strand of her hair.

Jani just smiled as she followed her mom. In a way, her dad was right. She wasn't mad he'd told her mom at all. The play was cool and maybe acting was her thing. That, and horses, of course.

Backstage was full of frantic activity. People rushed here and there, putting away props and costumes. Jani noticed that Hailey was backstage with her friend, Elaine. They were standing near a woman who looked more and more like Hailey as she removed her makeup.

When Hailey noticed Jani across the room, she waved. Jani waved back and was about to turn away, when she noticed Elaine glaring at her with angry eyes. What was wrong with her? She scowled back.

"Jani, this is our director, Mr. Wallace."

Jani turned to meet the man who might be directing her very first play, and for the next few minutes was totally entertained by the wiry, energetic man. When he rushed off to help someone move a couch – one of the props – Jani looked back. Hailey and Elaine were gone. It was probably just as well. Obviously, Elaine didn't want Jani talking to them. The way she'd looked at her – killer!

Jani found a comfy chair in the corner to wait. If only Penny hadn't procrastinated on her French homework and had been allowed to come tonight, the waiting wouldn't be so bad. Jani sighed. There was nothing to do but hope her mom wouldn't take too long getting ready to go.

HAILEY

"But mom, you have to tell Elaine I can't go tomorrow," Hailey said loud enough that her mom could hear her above the rain thundering against the windshield. "I'm going over to Jani's for a while and then I need to mow the lawn."

"The lawn is fine and you won't be at Jani's all day. You'll have time to go to the lake too, Hailey," said her mom, her voice cheerful and unaware. "You've been doing too much around home this summer. Its time to have some fun and go to the lake with your friends."

"But even if the lawn is okay, the garden needs to be weeded," Hailey said, then quickly added, "I mean, for money." She didn't want her mom to suspect her of anything, so she couldn't act too generous.

"You're saving for something?"

"No, I … I mean, yes." More lies.

"What?"

"I can't say. It's a secret."

Her mom looked over at her and smiled. "You can tell me, can't you?"

Quickly, Hailey searched her thoughts. What could she say that her mom would agree with? Not a kitten. She'd tried that last year and it hadn't worked. Maybe a new dress? Her mom would understand that. But she didn't even like dresses and she'd be forced to wear it.

"It's a surprise. For you." A brilliant stroke. How

could her mom say no to that? She couldn't. "So can I stay home tomorrow?" She glanced over at her mom to see a look of frozen horror on her face, her hands like claws clutching the steering wheel.

The car slid sideways, then lurched into the air – the engine screamed as it revved in space – and then everything started happening in slow motion.

Gliding forever through the darkness.

The river coming up to crash into the windshield.

Being thrown hard against her seatbelt.

Roaring water everywhere: rain pummeling the roof, the river flooding the car.

Her mom slumped over the steering wheel, not moving.

Struggling with the seatbelt so she could go for help.

Pushing the door open and the current rushing into the car, pinning her against the dashboard.

Somehow finding the strength to force her way out.

The current picking her up.

The car lights receding into the night as the river carried her away.

JANI

Jani had only been waiting two minutes when her dad called her. Miraculously, it was time to go.

The rain was falling heavier than ever when they left the theater. Jani's dad snapped open an umbrella and hurried into the downpour, leaving Jani and her mom waiting under the overhang. A minute later, he drove up in the car. Jani dove for the back seat, clipped on her seatbelt, and they were off.

The night seemed especially dark, the headlights hardly illuminating anything but rain and the lines on the road. As they drove, Jani closed her eyes. The roar of rain on the car roof, the fast rhythm of the windshield wipers, and the murmur of her mom and dad's voices joined into one great blur of soothing sound. She wanted the drive to last forever. She felt so safe and warm and content.

The voices stopped. The car slowed. Jani opened her eyes. "Why are we stopping?"

"Someone's parked beside the road ahead," said Jani's dad. "We're just seeing if they need help."

"I hope no one's in trouble," added Jani's mom.

Now Jani could see the flashing red lights ahead. Not ambulance lights or police car lights, but hazard lights from a car.

A dark form ran toward them, waving its arms.

"It's Beatrice," said Jani's mom recognizing her fellow actor.

Beatrice rushed to the driver's side window and Jani's dad wound it down. Rain blew in.

"Dave, Anna, thank goodness! Do you have your cell phone with you? We need to call 911."

Jani's mom was already reaching into her purse.

"What's wrong?"

"A car went into the river – I don't know whose it is."

"Stay here," Jani's dad instructed and opened his door. Jani watched, stunned, as his form was silhouetted in the headlights, running toward the river. Everything was happening so fast!

"Get inside, Beatrice," said Jani's mom. "Tell me what happened." She entered "9-1-1" into her phone, then pressed "Call."

Beatrice slid into the driver's seat, shut the car door, and rolled up the window. "There were taillights ahead of me and then they went into the river and just disappeared –"

"Hello? Yes, we have an emergency."

Jani reached for the door handle. She knew that Beatrice had been driving home alone because she'd driven off as Jani and her mom waited beneath the overhang – so that meant that Dad was out there by himself, wading through a river that was most likely flooding because of all the rain, looking for a car. As quietly as she could, she opened the door. The rain sound became louder and Jani glanced sharply at her mom, but with the phone plastered to her ear, she didn't seem to notice. Then Jani was out.

She left the door ajar behind her, afraid her mom would hear the click of it shutting, and raced in the direction her father had gone. Her mom would see her now because the headlights illuminated her, but it was too late. Jani could pretend to not hear her call above the sound of the rain and the river.

A bright flash jagged the sky as she ran past Beatrice's car. She stopped at the edge of the road where the ground started to slope toward the river below and cupped her hands to her mouth. "Dad!" Thunder exploded around her, rolling on and on like a giant coffee grinder in the sky. "Dad!" she shrieked, as soon as the rumble died down.

There was no response. Jani bent to touch the wet ground with her hands and slid down the dark gravelly bank. Almost immediately, her foot splashed into freezing water. The river was so high that it had covered the swamp that should've been there.

"Jani!"

Her mom's voice floated toward her through the rain. But she couldn't turn back. Not now. Not when her dad might need her help.

Another flash of lightening illuminated the current in front of her – and a dozen yards from the bank, the car, half buried in the water. Her dad was helping a figure from the driver's seat of the car. He was okay! More than okay. He was a hero!

She scrambled along the edge of the river, closer to where he would most likely exit the current. The bank near the partially submerged car was completely dark. She couldn't see anything as she crept down to the water – which meant her dad wouldn't be able to either. That's how she could help. She could call him to the nearest shore.

"Dad, this way. Come this way!"

"Jani?"

"I'm on the bank."

"Coming." He started splashing directly toward her. Closer and closer, and then water splashed against her shins. She held out her hand to feel wet cloth.

"Are you okay?"

Her dad didn't respond, he was breathing so heavily. Slowly he labored up the gravel incline to the road, Jani right behind him. When they reached the road, the headlights from the two cars illuminated the reason he was so slow – he was carrying the driver. A woman.

Gently he lowered the unconscious woman to the road. Her head fell back, and Jani gasped. There was blood on her face and more coming from her nose.

"Her nose is broken," Jani's dad explained. "Let's hope that's all that's wrong." He took off his jacket.

Suddenly Jani felt a deep chill that had nothing to do with the cold rain and wind. She recognized this woman. She looked different now, without the makeup and with blood on her face, but she was almost sure it was the same face she'd seen in the theater. She clutched her dad's shoulder. "Dad."

He didn't look up.

"Dad!"

"Not now, Jani." Carefully, he slid the bunched up jacket beneath the woman's head.

"Dad, you have to go back to the car."

"Not now, Jani!" His voice was harsh.

Jani stepped back. Her dad hardly ever yelled at her.

Jani's mom came rushing through the rain with Beatrice right behind her. A flashlight shone in her hand and a wool blanket hung over her arm. Jani had completely forgotten about the emergency kit in the trunk of the car.

"It's Elizabeth," said Jani's mom, falling to her knees beside the prone woman. "Is she…"

"She's alive. The ambulance is on its way?"

"It should be here soon." Jani's mom carefully spread the wool blanket over Elizabeth's unconscious form as Beatrice opened the small first aid kit from the car.

"Mom, we have to check the car," Jani said, her voice desperate. When her mom looked up at her confused, she added, "The wrecked car. This is Hailey's mom, right?"

"Who?" Jani's dad said sharply.

"Hailey. She was at the play. And Elaine may have been in the car too."

Identical looks of horror struck all three adults at once.

"Take the flashlight," said Jani's mom, shoving the light into her husband's hand.

Without a word, Jani's dad raced to the side of the road. He slid down the gravelly bank, and then frantic splashes came from the river. The light beam bobbed across the water.

Lightening flashed and Jani saw her dad in mid stride, like the still frame of a movie, lurching through the water toward the car. The flashlight beam touched the car just as the thunder started. It rumbled on forever as Jani watched the light bob behind the car, then shine on the back seat. Then the front passenger seat.

She couldn't breathe when her dad turned the flashlight away from the car to look at the river racing past it. She could tell the current was fast, even from the bank. At least it was only to her dad's thighs. But on Hailey it would be almost to her waist, and much deeper farther out. And if she was hurt, what chance did she have if she wasn't in the car?

"Hailey!" her dad bellowed. "Elaine!"

Jani put her hands to both sides of her mouth. "Hailey!" she screamed at the top of her lungs. "Elaine!"

Flashing lights! Sirens! Jani spun around to see the ambulance pull to a stop beside the women. Two ambulance attendants hurried to treat Hailey's mom.

Then the police arrived. Beatrice spoke a few words to them, and one of the two hurried over to Jani, while the other stayed to talk to Jani's mom.

"Are you sure there was a girl in the car?"

"No... I... I..."

A policewoman bent to look into Jani's eyes. "Just take your time. Tell me what you know."

"I saw that lady with Hailey at the play and thought how Hailey looks like her. I guessed she was Hailey's mom."

"How old is Hailey? What does she look like?"

"She's about ten, I guess. And she has long reddish brown hair and lots of freckles. And her friend, Elaine, she was with them at the play. I don't know if they were giving her a ride home or not."

The policeman approached them, his face drawn and white. "The woman is conscious now. She confirms that her daughter was with her."

"And no one else?"

"No. The other girl caught a ride home with someone else."

"Start the search," commanded the policewoman. "I'll call in the Search and Rescue Team to help."

Jani huddled in the back of the car for hours as the night wore on. More and more people arrived – police officers, divers, and people in hip waders – it seemed everyone was out searching for Hailey but her. She wasn't allowed. She tried to sleep but every time she closed her eyes, she imagined Hailey's face much like she'd seen it that afternoon. White with fear, the freckles standing out like spots of orange across her cheeks and nose.

The only thing that made her feel better was thinking

of Freedom and Keeta in their comfy barn. They would be sleeping now, their sweet breath slow and rhythmic. They'd be warm and unworried, feeling safe from the rain that continued to pound incessantly on and on and on – making the river even higher and faster and far more dangerous with each passing moment.

Poor Hailey!

The car door opened and Jani's mom slid into the driver's seat. She turned to gaze sympathetically at her daughter. "Are you okay, honey?"

"I'm fine," Jani lied. "Did they find her?"

"Not yet."

Two more tears slipped down her cheeks.

"I'm going to take you home. You need some rest."

"Where's Dad?"

"He's still helping in the search." She did up her seatbelt and started the car.

Jani fastened her seatbelt too. "Do they know what happened yet? Like why they went off the road?"

"The police think Elizabeth's car hydroplaned. That's when the tires start to skim across the top of the water on the road, instead of touching the road itself. Then she lost control." Her voice was shaky. "She was driving a little too fast for the road conditions."

"And Hailey?"

"They're not sure how she got in the river, but her car door was open. Maybe she tried to get out and the current swept her downstream. Thank goodness she was wearing her seatbelt. Otherwise she may have gone through the windshield, then been swept away. At least this way, she has a chance."

Jani reached down to double check that her seatbelt was securely fastened. "I saw her today, before the play.

She was telling me…" Jani couldn't continue. Emotion clogged her throat.

"Don't worry, honey. They'll find her."

"Yeah," sputtered Jani. She had to believe that. "Mom, can I sleep with you tonight?"

"I think that's a great idea. We can keep each other company."

FREEDOM

Freedom paced back and forth, past her dam and back again. Over and over. Something had happened. She could feel it in the vibrations of her body, in the valleys of her mind, in the deepest ravines of her heart.

The cold had come to the strange girl.

Keeta opened her eyes and nickered to her, and Freedom paused long enough to nuzzle her dam, then started walking again.

She needed to do something to help the girl, but what? She had to go somewhere, but where?

Keeta sighed and Freedom felt a twinge of sympathy for her dam. Keeta was worried about her. The mare had tried to get her to rest a number of times in the last few hours. At first, Freedom really made an effort to do what her dam wanted – but then, before she knew it, her hooves would be moving again, back and forth, back and forth, going over the same ground again and again, just like her thoughts in her mind.

What was happening to the child?

Tendrils of light slowly brightened the night outside the barn windows, then came the wet, cold light of day. There would be no sunrise this morning. The clouds were too thick, the rain too heavy. Every time she glanced out the window at the black clouds, she felt worse. Scared, even.

The little girl needed her, desperately, and here she was, locked inside her stall with nothing to do but pace.

Pace, and think. Think and pace.

HAILEY

She was so cold – or at least she thought she was cold. Her hands were so numb she wasn't sure, and she couldn't feel her feet at all. But she did feel frigid stones jabbing against her back. She turned her head and winced when her skull rubbed against rock. Her legs and arms too, ached with the sharp chill, and though she wasn't sure, she thought her foot was moving. Back and forth, back and forth, as if something was gently tugging on her shoe.

She opened her eyes. It was barely light – the kind of eerie grayness that meant morning hadn't fully arrived. Trees arched above her, and above them, large, dark clouds hung like swollen misty bags. A loud rushing roar smothered all sound except for one lone bird singing, somewhere nearby. And a chopping noise.

Where was she?

She struggled into a sitting position and saw water racing by in front of her. Her foot was caught in the current that sped over the gravel bar, and when she tried jerking it out, her leg wouldn't move. The muscles were too cold. She clutched at her leg with weak hands and somehow pulled her foot out of the river's grasp.

How had she gotten here? She didn't know this place. Had she come out of the river? Or was she walking along the bank when she slipped on the wet rocks and narrowly avoided falling into the current?

The person chopping wood back in the forest might know the answers. She could still hear the whack of an axe hitting wood.

"Hello?" Her voice was weak next to the river's surging clamor. No one would hear her from here. She needed to yell from some place quieter.

But to get away from the river, she had to get her legs working. Slowly, she started rubbing them. The rough denim made the skin on her hands feel raw. Of course that would be the first sensation to return – pain. She bent one leg at the knee, just a little at first, then moved it down and tried the other. So far, so good.

She tried bigger movements, with more reach. Her arms and legs burned as the feeling returned, but she didn't stop. Her efforts were paying off. Soon she'd be able to crawl away from the bank of this terrifying river. Even as she'd sat there, trying to mobilize herself, it had risen an inch.

When she felt ready, she turned onto her hands and knees and shuffled away from the water. Pinecones and stones jabbed at her palms, but she refused to let them slow her down. It was the dizziness that stopped her.

The next thing she knew, she was waking up again. Her cheek was pressed down against moss and twigs, and an ant waved its antennae at her an inch from her left eye. She heard the axe strike wood again.

"Hello? Can you hear me?" she called without lifting her head. She didn't want to move anymore. Every muscle in her body was either numb or on fire. At least the numb parts didn't hurt – yet.

There was no response to her call. She shuddered and closed her eyes. She had to get up and walk. Slowly, she sat up again, rubbing her head. There was a lump there, behind her right ear. So she must have slipped and hit her head. But what was she doing on the riverbank – everything about this place seemed completely unfamiliar.

There was one explanation: she might have come here with the person she heard chopping wood, then wandered off to explore. Surely, she wasn't out here alone. But why couldn't she remember?

She positioned her legs beneath herself and stood. She could feel her feet now, unfortunately. Her skin felt stiff, the soles of her feet patchy hot, her toes non-existent – but at least she could walk.

She took a step and was surprised when she didn't fall. Her strength was coming back quickly. Now which way had the chopping sound come from? The right?

It took ages to walk even a few yards, because she had to go so slowly. If only her body would start acting like her own, or there weren't quite so many things to avoid: roots, branches, twigs, bushes. If only she hadn't wandered away or done whatever she'd done… If only, if only, *if only*.

She came to the edge of the trees and stopped. An elderly man was there, on the other side of the clearing, his dark red coat bright against all the greens and browns of the forest. Even beneath these dark clouds, he stood out like a beacon as he picked up chopped wood from the ground and loaded it into a small cart.

"Hello," she called again, and the man froze. Straightened. Stared at her. "I fell and hit my head. I'm …" She stopped, her mouth still open. She couldn't remember her name. Abrupt fear lanced through her heart. Why couldn't she remember her own name?

The man was moving quickly toward her now. "Are you okay? Are you cold?"

The girl nodded.

"You fell in the river," he said, reaching her side. He whipped off his heavy coat and placed it gently around her shoulders.

"I'm not sure."

"Your clothes are wet."

The girl looked down surprised. They were. How had she not noticed? "I guess I did and somehow I got out again. I don't remember." She looked up at the man. He had a wrinkled comfortable face and kind eyes. "Do you know me?" she asked. "Do I know you?"

The man blinked in surprise. "What do you mean?"

"I can't remember who I am." She clutched the coat tight around herself. "You do know me, don't you?" she asked hopefully. If only he'd say yes, then she wouldn't feel so frightened, so vulnerable.

"We need to get you warmed up and under shelter before the rain starts again."

"But do I know you?" she asked again, stumbling back a step. Why wasn't he answering her question?

The man looked down at her, a strange expression on his face. Then he answered firmly. "Yes," he said. "I'm your grandfather."

"And why can't I remember?"

"You must be suffering from shock. And exposure too, I imagine. We need to get you someplace warm, and quick. Will you let me carry you?"

The girl pulled the coat tight around herself, letting the warmth soak into her skin like a healing balm. "Okay," she said. "But Grandpa, what's my name?"

For a moment, Grandpa looked like he was about to cry, then just as quickly, the expression was gone. It must have been her imagination. "Jenny," he said, his voice low.

The girl nodded. The name didn't seem remotely familiar and neither did this man, but then nothing did. And he was obviously her grandfather. Why else would he be in the woods with her? Why else would he act so worried about her?

She laid her head on his shoulder when he picked her up. Her eyes were already drooping, but she tried to fight the exhaustion. She wanted to see where home was, what it looked like. Maybe she'd recognize something there. But the warmth and his rhythmic stride and strong arms lulled her. She was safe now. There was no point in staying awake. She'd recognize everything later anyway.

JANI

Jani heard the clang of the coffeepot. Someone in the kitchen was making the morning coffee. She swung her legs out of her parents' bed and hurried to the kitchen. Her dad was standing by the sink. The early dawn light made him look far older than he had yesterday, or maybe it was just because he hadn't had any sleep that night. His face seemed as gray as the day outside and there were deep lines under his puffy eyes. He tried to smile at her as he moved to the table with his cup of coffee.

"Did you find her?"

"Not yet."

Jani slumped down on one of the kitchen chairs. "So that means –"

"She might still be okay. There's a chance."

Jani looked up at him hopefully. "Really?"

"Yeah," he whispered and quickly turned away. "We're going to start searching along the riverbank on horseback, motorbike, whatever we have available," he continued with his back to her. "I'd like to take Keeta if –"

"But I want to go too," Jani jumped up and hurried to the phone. "Maybe we can borrow a horse from Evergreen Stables. Keeta's too small for you anyway."

"We need to leave in less than an hour," he said, glancing at his watch.

Jani's mom strode into the room. "Just enough time to have some breakfast." She pulled a frying pan out of the cupboard, as Jani went to the phone. "How many eggs do you guys want?"

When neither Jani nor her dad answered, she poured oil into the pan and turned the stove element to med-low. Jani dialed the stables and listened to the phone ring.

A man's voice answered the phone finally. "Evergreen Stables. Hello?"

"Hello, Mr. Regan? This is Jani Preston. Sorry to wake you but it's an emergency. We're wondering if you have a horse we can borrow for the search."

"Two horses, Jani," her mom said from behind her.

"I mean two horses, one for each of my parents. They both know a bit about riding."

When she hung up the phone, Jani turned to her mom and dad. "He said yes, and that he'll take them over to Wilson's for you – that's where everyone's meeting – and he'll saddle them up, so they're ready for you when you get there."

"That really helps," said Jani's mom.

"He's joining the search too, and so is Penny. She's already there, getting Sunny ready."

"That'll give you half an hour to rest, Dave. Why don't you go get some sleep?"

Jani's dad kept staring down into his coffee.

"Dave!"

He started, then looked up, bleary eyed. "Yeah?"

"You have half an hour to sleep. Go," said Jani's mom, leaving no room for argument. She cracked an egg into the pan. "I'll throw your eggs in a bun; you can eat in the car on the way over."

Jani's dad nodded and lumbered from the room.

"I'll go get Keeta ready," said Jani.

"Be back in fifteen minutes. You need to eat too," her

mom said, her voice still firm. Jani nodded. There was no time to argue, even though she really didn't feel very hungry. She pulled on her jacket, then slipped a raincoat overtop, and headed out the back door. A gust of wind sent a splat of rain straight into her face.

Stepping into the barn was like entering another world, a world of peace and tranquility – or at least Keeta looked calm as she leaned over the stall door. Jani gave her a quick rub on the forehead before hurrying past to the feed room to get some oats. She was glad she'd thought to give Keeta some extra feed last night. There was still some hay in her manger. The mare wouldn't miss her breakfast.

Swift brush strokes over Keeta's red and white body made her gleam in the low light. When Jani was done, she tried to groom Freedom, but soon stopped. The filly was too agitated to hold still.

"You know there's something wrong, don't you, girl?" Jani murmured. "It's Hailey, she's gone. We're going to go find her." Her speech faltered as Freedom stared at her, understanding seeming to radiate from her clear, blue eyes. "But you know all that."

Hearing her own words made Jani frown. With Freedom's history, there was no doubt that she was an amazing horse. Jani had first discovered her as a dark spirit, consumed with hatred and trapped in the barn that had once stood on their property. After she and Penny helped the ghost forgive the past and leave the barn, Freedom had proved her further uniqueness by coming back to Jani as a living horse: Keeta's foal. But no matter how remarkable Freedom was, she was still a horse. And she, Jani, was being silly. There was no way Freedom could know any of what had happened.

By the time the mare finished her oats, both horses were ready to go. Jani gave them both a quick kiss on the nose. "Be back soon, guys," she said as she slipped out of the stall and tried to shut the door behind her. She turned back when the door wouldn't close. Freedom was trying to squeeze out behind her. Patiently, Jani pushed the filly back into the stall.

"We'll be on our way soon enough, Freedom," she said as the latch caught. "By the end of the day, you'll be longing for your nice warm stall. Unless we find her sooner." A pause. "We have to find her sooner."

HAILEY

The girl opened her eyes to see a dirty ceiling. Cobwebs drooped in the corner above her head – or were they spider webs? She shuddered. For some odd reason, that was one thing she did remember. She hated spiders.

She turned her head to take in the room, hoping that she'd recognize something. Anything. A shabby dresser squatted against the wall across from the bed and an old chair languished beside it. Her jacket hung on the back of it.

The girl rubbed her fingers against her stomach under the covers, then moved her hand down to touch her legs. Thank goodness, she was still wearing her damp clothes. Having her grandpa carry her home was one thing, but she didn't want him undressing her like she was a little kid. That would be too embarrassing.

However there was no reason to stay in her damp clothes now. She should have some clean, dry ones here somewhere, in a suitcase if she was just visiting or in the chest of drawers if she lived here. Or maybe in the closet.

She sat up in bed, groaned, and lay back again. The dizziness was back in full force, only this time she felt slightly nauseous too.

She didn't need to get changed yet anyway. The heavy quilt was keeping her toasty warm. She closed her eyes. If she slept a bit longer, her clothes might even dry by the time she woke again. And hopefully, she'd feel better too. Maybe her memory would come back. She hated the emptiness of not knowing who she was, other than a granddaughter. Her own name didn't even feel familiar, but she thought she could feel memories lingering just below the surface of her conscious mind, like a word on the tip of her tongue that refused to be spoken. That meant her memories would come back to her, right?

Did she have a mom and dad? Brothers and sisters? She felt like she did.

"Grandpa?" she called, hoping he was nearby. He should be able to answer her questions. Then maybe she'd remember.

But there was no response. He'd probably gone back to the woods to get the firewood he'd chopped.

The girl closed her eyes again. She'd ask her questions as soon as he got home, and in the meantime, she'd sleep. She was still amazingly tired. That was odd, considering she felt she'd already slept for days.

JANI

Jani and Penny rode at the back of the search party so that Jani could keep Freedom away from the other horses. Keeta didn't like strange horses near her foal, and Jani too found it stressful when they flocked around her black filly. It was as if Freedom was equine royalty and they all wanted to touch her or bask in her attention. Even Penny had noticed it and occasionally called the filly Her Majesty. Freedom, of course, was not the least bit intimidated, and encouraged the attention from other horses as much as possible.

"Wow." The word slipped from Penny's mouth as they rode around a corner in the road. Her palomino gelding, Sunny, raised his head and snorted.

Jani's eyes widened. The old logging road met up with the bridge here – and beneath the wooden structure, the river looked more terrifying and dangerous than she'd ever seen it. The brown, sullen current was even with the bank and unless it stopped rising very soon, the river was going to break free to submerge the surrounding land, no doubt ripping out trees and bushes, and drowning all the herbs on the forest floor. The thought that Hailey might be caught in the terrible maelstrom was unbearable.

"I hope the bridge is safe," Penny said.

"Me too," said Jani. She kept a sharp eye ahead as the first two riders reached it. Their horses stared with bugged eyes at the current on either side and quickly minced across the bridge. The other riders followed, their horses cautiously stepping onto the bridge and walking slowly until they were halfway across, then racing the rest of the way across the wooden expanse.

Only one horse balked – Elaine's horse, Rain Shadow. Elaine didn't push the big gelding, but let him stand and sniff at the bridge as the others rode past them. After four horses had passed, Rain Shadow decided he could brave the bridge too.

When it was Jani and Penny's turn, Jani shortened the lead rope that kept Freedom near them. The filly kept close behind Keeta, her expressive blue eyes looking at the current with concern. "Don't worry, Freedom," Jani murmured. "Just stay close to Keeta." As if she understood Jani's words, the foal crowded even closer to her dam.

When they reached the other side of the bridge, the search party divided into their prearranged groups of three. Jani and Penny were slated to ride with her dad along the river to the right of the bridge.

Jani's mom was in Elaine's and Mr. Regan's group. Their plan was to trot ahead along the old dirt road and trails until they were about two miles downstream. Then they would hang some flagging tape next to the riverbank where they started their search, and Jani's group would search to the bright tape. The other two groups were to go to the left, and were going to divide the four miles of river between them before they reached the town, then widen their search on the way back to the bridge. Motorbike riders and hikers were already searching the opposite side of the river.

"Elaine, are you okay?" Jani asked, riding up to Hailey's best friend.

Elaine's face was pale, her eyes large and sorrowful. She nodded, obviously unable to speak. How terrible she must feel with her best friend missing and possibly drowned. This would be an absolute nightmare for her.

"We'll all do our best to find her," added Jani, thinking she should say something positive. Elaine nodded again, and Jani noticed fresh tears running down her cheeks.

Not knowing what else to say, Jani reined Keeta back to her own group. She waved to her mom before her mom trotted away on Champagne, the beautiful cremello mare that Mr. Regan had lent her. Elaine glanced at Jani as she reined Rain Shadow to follow Champagne and Jani gave her a tentative wave. Miserably, Elaine waved back.

"Ready, girls?" asked Jani's dad, riding up to them on a big chestnut gelding named Apollo. He was the perfect horse for her dad to ride: calm, sensible, and very good in the bush. His rider, however inexperienced, would be very well taken care of. Like so many of the other horses, he seemed drawn to Freedom, and edged toward her until Keeta laid her ears back at him.

"I'm ready," said Penny.

"Me too." Jani reached down to unclip the foal's lead rope. Freedom could be a valuable asset in the search. She'd notice things that the humans might miss and that the other horses wouldn't be free to investigate because of their riders.

"Remember, we're looking for anything unusual or out of place," instructed Jani's dad. "A scrap of cloth, a shoe, tracks leaving the river, anything."

"Mr. Preston?" asked Penny, as they rode into the forest at the side of the road. "Do you think we'll find her?"

"I do."

Jani straightened when she heard the conviction in her

father's voice. There was something in his strong answer that gave her hope, even though logically it seemed there was little hope. The river was too high, too wild.

"I'll ride closest to the river," Jani's dad said. "Penny you ride beside me, about ten yards over. Jani you ride ten yards farther on and we'll all ride parallel to each other."

"Okay," said Penny. She reined Sunny away from Apollo.

"Come on, Freedom," Jani said and guided Keeta farther into the woods.

The going was rough and sometimes Jani lost sight of Penny and her dad behind bushes and trees, even though they were only a short distance away. She was glad she had Freedom to help her look. It was tough seeing everything she needed to see in all that undergrowth. What if Hailey had crawled from the river and laid down right on the other side of that fallen log? What if she'd fallen into that mossy hole?

Freedom moved like a dark shadow beneath the trees, back and forth, checking behind every obstacle, in every crevice. Once Jani even noticed her looking up at the treetops. She had to know they were searching for something, even though she couldn't possibly know what. Either that or her curiosity was normal for young horses – Jani had never owned a foal before, so she wasn't sure which.

Slowly, they made their way along the river, keeping each other updated although there was nothing to report but trees, bushes, rocks, moss, and the occasional animal trail that looked untouched by human feet. Once Jani saw a soft drink can – how it got so deep in the forest, she had no idea – but she didn't bother mentioning it. The can was almost completely covered by needles and other tree litter, and the exposed part was faded. Obviously it had been there a long time. And besides, Freedom ignored it so it couldn't be important.

They'd been searching for almost an hour when Jani suddenly noticed that the filly was missing. "Freedom!" She pulled Keeta to a halt.

"What's happening, Jani?" Jani's dad yelled.

"Is Freedom with you? Can you see her?"

"She didn't come this way."

"Or past me," added Penny. She stopped Sunny and looked over to Jani with a worried face.

"Freedom!"

Keeta neighed loudly, calling Freedom to her. The bushes crackled and Jani spun the mare around to face the river – but it was only her dad riding into view from the other side of a big tree.

"Go find her, Jani. And put a rope on her. We don't have any time to waste." He glanced up at the sky.

Jani looked up too. Beyond the treetops, the cloud ceiling seemed even lower and was definitely darker. She reined Keeta deeper into the woods. The mare needed no encouragement. She was just as worried for her foal as Jani was.

"Freedom!" When there was no response again, Jani yelled over her shoulder, "You go ahead with the search. I'll get her and catch up."

Keeta sprung into a fast trot and Jani didn't hear her dad's or Penny's response. The mare's head was high as she wove through the trees. Jani looked down. Keeta had found a wild animal trail.

Thirty seconds later, they broke out of the trees and into a clearing. Freedom stood before them, sniffing the firewood scattered over the ground.

Keeta relaxed the moment she saw the errant foal, but

Jani kept her trotting until they reached the filly. "Come on, Freedom. Dad and Penny are waiting," she said and slid from the saddle, the lead rope in her hand. She patted the ebony neck. "Someone gets their firewood for the winter here, that's all."

She clipped the lead rope to the filly's halter and led her back to her dam, then mounted the mare again. Together, they retraced their steps along the animal trail. Jani's dad and Penny were waiting just where she'd left them and quickly she explained where she'd found Freedom.

"Was the wood a bright color where it was split?" asked Jani's dad.

Jani shrugged. "I guess."

"Then it's freshly chopped. Let's go check it out."

Before following Penny and her dad, Jani bent down to pat Freedom's neck and unclip her lead rope. "It looks like you might be right, Freedom."

The filly nickered at her, then turned to follow the others.

A couple of minutes later, they were back in the clearing. Jani's dad looked down at the wood pieces, then his gaze moved to the half full handcart. "Someone was loading wood and then left everything," he said. "I wonder why?"

"Maybe they went home for lunch," suggested Jani.

"But it would've taken only a few more minutes to finish loading the cart and then they could've taken a load of wood home with them," said Penny.

"They have to live nearby," added Jani's dad. "That's not something anyone would want to pull for any great distance."

"Maybe it's Joe's."

"Who?" Jani and her dad asked together.

"Joe," Penny repeated. "He lives out here somewhere. I'm not sure where exactly but he's like a hermit or something."

"I think I've heard about him," said Jani's dad, rubbing his chin. "He only comes into town a couple times a year to shop for supplies and the rest of the time he stays in the bush. You say he lives near here?"

"Somewhere around here. I've never been to his house or anything. And I don't think he was always a hermit. He used to be married and I think they had a daughter, but then his wife died and his daughter… well, I don't remember what happened to her. It was a long time ago." When Jani looked at her with raised eyebrows, obviously impressed, Penny shrugged. "It's a small town. Everyone knows everything about everyone else. Or they think they do anyway."

Keeta shifted nervously beneath Jani, who automatically looked about for Freedom. She was walking away from them, down a rough track through the woods. "Maybe that's the way to Joe's house," she said and pointed. "Maybe he found Hailey and that's why he didn't finish loading up the wood he chopped."

"We should talk to him," said Jani's dad. He turned Apollo to follow Freedom, and Jani and Penny fell in behind.

The rough trail became more well trodden the farther they traveled along it and soon the horses were trotting. Freedom stopped for a moment to sniff at the ground and Apollo trotted sedately past her. When the filly tried to take the lead once more, the gelding warned her back.

Jani almost laughed aloud when Freedom tried to rush past Apollo's massive hindquarters for the third time and he switched his long red tail in her face. Freedom kicked the air with frustration. One thing was certain about Jani's intrepid filly: she certainly didn't like being told what to do! Even though she was now trotting along behind the gelding, acting like she was perfectly content to follow him forever, Jani knew she was just waiting for her chance to spring past him.

They trotted and loped along for five minutes, then broke out of the trees and onto a weedy, narrow road. Jani's dad turned Apollo to the right and they continued around a couple of corners until the road ended in a small field. Jani didn't notice there was a fence by the trees surrounding the pasture until they were through the open gate.

Freedom raced around Apollo and curved toward a cabin framed by a fenced vegetable garden with a small garage on one side and fruit trees on the other. It looked like Joe lived off the land as much as possible – but then he'd have to if he only came into town a couple times a year.

"Hello! Anyone home?" Jani's dad called.

Movement in the garage caught Jani's eye as a man straightened from under the hood of an ancient looking truck. He wiped his hands on a rag as they rode closer, then strode toward them. "I bet I know why you folks are…"

Abruptly, the man stopped short and his mouth fell open. His eyes looked as if they were going to bug out of his head.

Freedom reared up at the head of the group and claimed the air with a loud scream, then struck out with her small hooves.

Joe ran toward his house.

"Wait!" called Jani's dad and asked Apollo to trot after the man – but Joe had already sprung up the porch steps. Already wrenched open the door. Already slammed it behind him!

"What's wrong with him?" Jani asked Penny as her dad rode closer to the cabin. She could hear him calling to the man inside.

"I don't know," Penny admitted. "I never heard anything about him being crazy."

Jani's dad dismounted from Apollo, then walked up the porch steps and knocked on the door. The big gelding took the opportunity to crop the grass in front of the building.

"Freedom knew something was wrong. That's why she started acting all funny." Jani reached down to stroke the filly's neck. "Hey, she's shaking."

"Really? That's weird," said Penny, then inhaled sharply. "What if he's crazy *and* he's found Hailey?"

Jani straightened on Keeta's back, words of horror stuck in her throat. That would be beyond terrible!

"Okay, sorry to bother you." Jani heard her dad call to the house. "If you see anyone fitting her description, just let us know."

There was a muffled reply, but Jani and Penny were too far away to hear the words. Then Jani's dad was riding back toward them.

"What'd he say, Dad?"

Jani's dad frowned. "He hasn't seen anyone."

"So why'd he freak like that?"

"I don't know. Maybe we just surprised him. He can't be used to seeing anyone out here, let alone strangers."

Jani looked at Penny to see her friend slightly shake her head. So they were in agreement. Joe's over-the-top reaction couldn't have been a simple surprise. "I think we should get the police to check his house."

"They wouldn't be allowed to. There's no evidence he's done anything to Hailey."

"But Freedom doesn't like him."

"Ah yes, the brilliant Freedom," Jani's dad said. "She was simply reacting to his surprise, nothing more."

"But –"

"Come on. Let's get back to the river," interrupted Jani's dad. "We've wasted enough time here." Almost as an afterthought he added, "But it was a great idea to check with Joe, Jani. I wish he had seen her."

He asked Apollo to trot and Penny followed, but Jani held Keeta back for a moment. She looked back at Joe's cabin, searching the curtained windows for movement, for any sign of life.

She sighed and reached down to stroke Freedom, still pressed close to her dam.

Jani didn't know about Joe. He might be completely innocent. He might be just a crazy old guy. But she knew Freedom; she wasn't simply overreacting to Joe's surprise. The filly was frightened – and she wouldn't be scared unless there was a reason. A good reason.

FREEDOM

Freedom relaxed a bit more with every step they took away from the Monster Man's house. She remembered him. She'd met him before, in her life before Jani, when she was a wild one.

He was dangerous!

He ensnared others!

He betrayed those who trusted him!

She'd learned about him not only from her own experiences, back when she was a mustang, but also from her friend, Gentle One. As Freedom had lain dying, he'd forcefully carried Gentle One away from Freedom's side, cruelly separating them.

Freedom hung her head. Most of the time, the memories from that life were like looking into a dark pool, but for some reason seeing the Monster Man had brought them crashing back. He was older now, much older, but still she recognized him. She'd always recognize him.

There was only one good thing about Monster Man: his daughter, Gentle One. Freedom had never known the girl's human name, so she'd named her herself, and Gentle One suited her perfectly.

Freedom first met Gentle One when she was a young foal, too young to realize that swamps were dangerous, and had foolishly ventured into a bog and become stuck. At first, when the human appeared, Freedom was terrified, but Gentle One took a long time to approach and made soothing noises the whole while. Then she pulled her from the mud with a long snake that Freedom now understood was a rope.

After Gentle One saved her, Freedom allowed her to come near. She learned to enjoy listening to the human's sounds – her speech and singing. She learned to trust Gentle One's calm presence.

And then Monster Man betrayed them both, first Freedom and then his daughter.

What had become of her beautiful, tenderhearted friend? She hadn't sensed her anywhere near Monster Man's house. What had he done to her, after he ripped her away from Freedom's side? Had he hurt her even more? And was he about to do the same to the girl they were searching for – the girl that Jani called Hailey? For Freedom had no doubt she was inside Monster Man's house. She'd felt Hailey's *need* radiating from the house like an unseen light.

The small horse snorted. She had to go back. Though the idea of being near that terrible human made her quake with terror, she knew she had to face him. It was the right thing to do, to battle her fear. Hailey needed her, just like Gentle One had needed her. And this time she wasn't about to let Monster Man win.

HAILEY

The voices in the girl's dream changed. They started saying things she wasn't expecting them to say, things that weren't in context with the rest of her dream. In fact, they were ruining a perfectly lovely vision, one where she was jumping from a blue cloud to a pink cloud to a green cloud as she followed a purple spotted kitten that giggled just like… someone she knew well. Her best friend?

Then the voices stopped. Finally. She leapt from the green cloud to a red one and was about to hop to yellow when a knocking sound, loud and stiff, interrupted her dream.

"Jenny?"

Jenny? Oh, right…

How could one's own name seem so unfamiliar?

Blinking away the last shreds of sleep, the girl opened her eyes. "Yeah?"

The door opened and her grandfather leaned in. He looked like he hadn't combed his hair or shaved in a week and his shirt was filthy, marred with greasy patches.

"Jenny, how are you feeling?"

"I'm fine, Grandpa. Just really tired, that's all."

"Okay. I'll let you sleep then." But instead of leaving, he cleared his throat. Obviously, he had more to say.

"Yeah?" she asked, hoping to encourage him. He was taking so long and it was taking serious effort just keeping her eyes open.

"I, uh, just wanted to let you know that I'm working

on the truck. As soon as it's fixed, I'll take you to the hospital. We need to have you examined, in case you hit your head when you fell."

"Sure," she agreed, and rolled over to face the wall. She cuddled into the softness of the pillow. Whether he took her to the hospital or not was unimportant, as long as it was later and he left her alone right now. Couldn't he tell she was tired?

Still, the door behind her didn't close. How did he expect her to relax with him watching her?

"What else, Grandpa?" she said to the wall.

"Nothing." Another long pause. "Well, except, uh, I was wondering, you didn't hear anything just now, did you?"

"Like what?"

"Oh, nothing important." Another long pause. "Just anything unusual, that's all."

The girl rolled back and stared at him from under drooping eyelids. "What do you mean, *unusual*?"

"Nothing. Nothing," he said hurriedly. "Sorry to bother you. Just get some rest." He snapped his head back out of sight and closed the door softly behind him.

Finally. The girl closed her eyes and tried to relax.

But now she couldn't. His question burrowed into her drowsiness like a mole digging its way through soft ground. What did he mean, had she heard anything unusual? She hadn't heard anything at all – except for some voices as she was waking up. But what was unusual about voices?

Nothing.

But Grandpa's worried, she reasoned. *So if the only thing I heard was voices, then the unusual thing has to be… those voices. Maybe he's worried that I overheard something I shouldn't.*

She opened her eyes reluctantly. The problem was that she really didn't remember what the voices said. She heard the main door to the house shut and guessed her grandfather had gone back outside, probably to work on the truck as he'd told her.

She sat up. Immediately a wall of nauseating dizziness assaulted her again. She hugged her knees to her chest and prepared to wait it out. If she just sat still...

She thought about the voices some more. True she couldn't remember the words, but she was sure they'd belonged to two men. She could remember that much. Her grandfather and a stranger.

The dizziness diminished a little but still she waited. The off-kilter feeling was so familiar, she was sure she'd felt it before. It was a memory, of sorts. The dizziness *meant* something. If only she could remember what.

JANI

They were halfway back to the river, when Freedom stopped, turned, and headed resolutely back along the trail. "Dad, just a sec. Freedom's taking off again!"

Jani's dad pulled Apollo to a halt. "Put a rope on her, Jani. I mean it. We can't keep wasting time like this."

"Sorry." Jani turned Keeta and rode after Freedom. "I'll catch her and be right back. You keep searching. Penny and I can catch up to you in a couple of minutes," she said, looking meaningfully at her friend.

"Okay, I'll be moving slowly if I have to check your sections too, so I won't be far ahead. But hurry." His voice broached no room for argument.

Jani asked Keeta to trot and Penny and Sunny trotted along behind her as they went back along the trail toward Joe's house. The filly was already out of sight. They rounded two corners before they came across her black rump moving away from them. Jani slowed Keeta to a walk and Penny drew Sunny alongside her, an eager expression on her face.

"Thank goodness for Her Majesty."

"Yeah, I'd hate to have to come back at night or something."

Penny laughed. "You would do that, wouldn't you? You're funny."

"What do you mean, *me*? You're just as bad as I am."

"Shhh. We're getting close."

HAILEY

The dizziness finally abated enough that the girl felt she could move to the edge of her bed. Slowly, with her hand on the headboard, she stood. So far, so good. As long as she didn't make a sudden movement, she'd be okay. She almost smiled, but winced instead. The last thing she'd be doing was making any sudden movements. Now that she was warm and the numbness of sleep had left her mind, she felt battered and bruised beyond belief – further scary evidence that she'd actually fallen into the river.

She shuffled to the window and pulled back the heavy curtains. A field stretched out in front of the house and she could see a distant gate and fence. No garage – not that it mattered. Her grandfather wasn't in it. He was walking slowly, wearily, away from the house.

He didn't go far. When he reached the gate, he swung it shut and then put a chain around the gatepost. Why would he be locking the gate? Could it have something to do with the voices she'd heard, the ones he was worried about?

If only she could remember what they'd said.

When he turned toward the house, she pulled away, letting the curtains fall closed. Immediately, she felt guilty. Why was she so reluctant to let him see her watching him? He was her grandfather. He wouldn't do anything to hurt her. Yet her hands seemed to have a will of their own, refusing to open the curtains and wave to him.

Instead, she leaned close and peered out through a

narrow gap in the cloth. There he was, stomping back toward the house. As he drew nearer, she could see the worry lines etched on his grizzled forehead. Something was bothering him – a lot.

If only her memory would return …

She shambled back toward the bed, but changed direction halfway there. She needed a drink. She'd just grab a glass of water from the kitchen and then she'd be off to dreamland again. Sleep – that was the best thing she could do right now. As soon as she caught up on her rest, she'd not only feel better, but she'd probably start remembering things as well. And then, hopefully, some of these irritating mysteries would be solved.

JANI

They turned their horses onto the narrow road and rounded the last corner just in time to see Joe walking back toward his house, the massive wooden gate between him and them closed, chained, and padlocked. She glanced around. Where was Freedom? They'd only been seconds behind the filly and yet she'd disappeared.

"Jani," Penny hissed. Jani turned to see Penny pointing to the filly's rump poking out from behind a tree at the side of the road. Jani shook her head in amazement – though she and Penny could see part of Freedom, the filly would've been completely hidden from Joe while he was locking the gate.

Quietly, the two girls turned the horses back down the road, and Freedom crept silently from her station behind the tree to follow them. Once they were safely out of sight around the bend, Jani pulled Keeta to a stop.

"I think we should check the house," she whispered, though there was no way Joe could hear them now.

Penny blinked. "While he's there?"

"He was working on his truck in the garage before. Maybe he'll go back to doing that," she said, dismounting. She led Keeta to the side of the muddy road, tied her to a branch just higher than her head, and patted her shoulder.

Penny hadn't dismounted yet. "It's going to be even harder to get up to the house if he's in that garage. It only has three walls."

"You don't have to come."

Penny gave an exaggerated sigh. "There's only one problem with staying here. I'm getting tired of playing the sensible one. It's boring always being reasonable."

"Sensible? Reasonable? I thought we were talking about you?"

"Hey, I'm *usually* sensible," Penny protested as she dismounted. "But right now it doesn't make any sense to be sensible, not when Hailey might be locked in his house. And besides, there's no way I'm going to stay here while you hog all the excitement."

Jani laughed quietly. "You stay here, Freedom," she murmured to the filly as Penny secured Sunny to a tree near Keeta. "There's nothing more you can do now." She patted the filly before she and Penny crept into the woods.

Soon, they were back near the fence, the field stretching away to their right. Jani stopped and stared at the house and garage. She'd been right. Joe was bent over the truck engine and the sound of metal clanging against metal reached her ears.

"Sounds like he's trying to beat it into submission," Penny whispered beside her.

They moved quietly along the fence line. When the view of the garage was completely blocked by the house, Jani and Penny climbed through the rustic pole fence and ran as fast as they could toward the building. The cabin drew nearer and nearer. They were past the fruit trees. Just a few more steps – and finally they were there, pressing their backs against the log wall. Safe. For now anyway.

When she'd caught her breath, Jani held out her leg to display her jeans, soaked from the knee down. "Look," she panted. "Dad's going to know we got off the horses."

"Maybe he'll think we were chasing Freedom," Penny said hopefully.

Jani shook her head. "Not a chance. He knows us too well."

"Then we should hurry before he realizes we're taking too long and comes back to catch us peering in windows."

"Good idea. You go look through all those windows," Jani said, pointing toward the back of the house. "And I'll check the others. We'll meet back here."

"Okay."

Jani hurried to her left and stopped at the first window. It was covered with a thick curtain and try as she might, she couldn't see anything of the room behind it.

Before moving on, she looked for Penny but her friend had already gone around the back of the house. Jani moved the last steps to the corner and leaned cautiously around to peer at the front. A shabby porch clung to the house with a window perched on either side of it – two more to check.

The only problem was, if Joe came out of the garage, he'd see her in a heartbeat. And if he was faster than her, he might catch her. She would be in big trouble then!

Jani took a deep breath. She had no choice. Penny was checking the other windows, and it was her responsibility to check these, especially since she didn't even *claim* to be sensible. She dropped to her hands and knees and crawled around the corner of the house, keeping close to the dark, rain soaked logs and staring hard at the garage doorway as she scuttled forward.

At long last, she reached the first window and looked up. Good. It wasn't too high. She should be able to see just over the sill. Slowly, slowly she rose to her feet and straightened, stretched. She imagined Joe's unfriendly eyes boring into her back, into her skull – but she had to do it. Hailey might be in there, needing her help.

Heavy dark red curtains covered the window. Jani scowled. This was too irritating! She was just reaching to tap on the window, in case Hailey was inside to hear her, when she heard the rifle shot.

Her heartbeat boomed in her ears. For a moment she couldn't breathe – and then she was running, running, running. The shot was too far away to be done by Joe, but the timing of it was beyond terrible. She had no doubt he would come out of the garage to look around. Who wouldn't? And if she didn't make it around the corner in time, he would see her!

HAILEY

The girl found a chipped cup and looked for a tap. There wasn't one. And no fridge to hold any juice or milk either. Weird. Unless she wasn't in the kitchen. But there was an old-fashioned wood cook stove, a sink and cupboards, even a table and two chairs next to the window. She had to be in the right room. She opened one of the cupboard doors. Yes, there were some pots and a huge frying pan. So all she needed to do was find where Grandpa kept his drinking water.

She opened another cupboard – just dried beans, a bag of rice, and some onions, carrots, and potatoes. It all looked so gross. Is this what she normally ate? If so, no wonder she wanted to forget about it.

Quickly, she checked the rest of the smaller cupboards – there weren't many so it didn't take long – and finally moved on to the tall cupboard against the outside wall. She pulled the door open to find a big pot, full of water, with a ladle hanging on the side. How peculiar. And behind the pot, a screened hole to the outside. What was that for?

She scooped up water without bothering with the ladle and gulped down the cool liquid. It tasted heavenly on her lips, in her mouth, in her dry, parched throat. When the water was gone, she scooped up more and drank a second cup, then refilled it once again. She shivered before closing the door – the air inside the cupboard was cold. Then she understood: that was what the screened opening was for, to let cool air from outside into the cupboard. This cupboard was an old fashioned fridge. Which meant – she looked up at the ceiling to see no light fixtures – there was no electricity in the house. Weird!

She carried her full cup into the adjoining room. A quick side trip before going back to bed wouldn't hurt. Maybe she'd even find something to stimulate her memories.

An old, comfy looking chair sat beside a wood stove in the small room and ancient looking books lined the shelves against one wall. Dark red curtains covered the one window, making the room appear cave-like and cozy.

So this was the living room. The girl held one hand above the stove to feel the heat. It was much warmer in here than her bedroom. Maybe she should curl up in the big chair and sleep in front of the stove.

Five framed photographs, lining a shelf near the chair, caught her gaze. She put her cup down on the shelf and eagerly reached for the nearest. A woman in her twenties stared back at her. She didn't look at all familiar.

The second photo contained three people: the same woman, a bit older this time, with a man who was obviously Grandpa before he'd gotten old. A ten-year-old girl stood with them and all three smiled at the camera.

The girl put the second photo back in place and quickly scanned the three remaining images. All of the photographs were old. The most recent one showed the girl – who might be her mother – as a young teenager, but there were no photos of the girl as a grown up. There were no photos of the woman – her grandmother? – getting older.

"Are you my mom?" She touched the teenaged girl's face with a hesitant finger, then lifted the photo from the

shelf and moved toward the silver framed mirror on the wall. She looked at herself in the glass, drinking in her own features. She looked… right. Though she couldn't have described her own appearance before looking in the mirror, she looked exactly the way she expected to look – familiar – right down to the unfortunate freckles.

Relieved, she moved closer to the window where the light from around the curtain edge further illuminated the old photograph's surface. The girl didn't look at all like her. Her hair was a different color, her face shape was different, her eyes rounder, her nose straighter.

A sudden sound, like a gunshot, came from outside, faint and far away, and she pushed the curtain to the side to look out.

There was a flash of blue below the window – someone was there! She pushed up next to the glass and stared downward, but saw nothing more. Yet *another* strange happening. Things would be so much simpler if she could just remember. Then she might know who had a habit of looking through her windows.

The girl moved methodically to the shelf and put the photo back in exactly the same place, then picked up her glass and wiped away the ring of water it left on the shelf.

She was halfway back to her room before she understood what she'd seen on the shelf – or rather, what she *hadn't* seen. No pictures of her. Not one. A shiver jittered up her backbone and made the back of her neck prickle. If this man really was her grandfather, wouldn't he have pictures of her on his shelf too?

JANI

Jani skidded around the corner of the house, almost collided with Penny, then together they raced back across the field. A minute later, they were through the fence and safely hidden in the forest's bushy undergrowth.

Jani's breath came in gasps as she stared back at the house. Joe was walking toward his front door. He seemed oblivious, thank goodness.

"That was so close," whispered Penny. A bird cried overhead.

Though he was too far away to hear Penny's voice, the bird's call must have meant something to Joe. He stopped short and looked directly toward them.

Jani clutched Penny's arm. This was too creepy. "Let's go back to the horses."

Together, the two girls crept away from the fence and deeper into the forest. They wound their way through the trees, ducking branches and dodging around bushes.

"Did you see anything?" Jani asked as soon as they reached Keeta, Sunny, and Freedom. She gave Keeta a hug and felt her heart calm. She breathed deep.

"No. Just a couple of empty bedrooms. It looked pretty depressing actually."

Jani grimaced. She'd been so sure they'd find Hailey there. Maybe Freedom's antics really had meant nothing. "Two of my windows had curtains over them, and I didn't have time to see through the farthest front window." She pulled away from Keeta and scratched Freedom on her poll.

"You went in front?" Penny sounded incredulous.

"Of course, I went in front," Jani said, nonchalantly. Penny didn't need to know she'd been terrified the entire time.

"But what if he came out of the garage? He would've seen you."

Jani shrugged. "It was no big deal. Until that gunshot went off, anyway."

"Yeah, what was *that*?" Penny untied Sunny's reins and put them over his neck.

"I didn't want to hang around to find out," said Jani, climbing to Keeta's back.

"Me neither. I hope everyone's okay." Penny mounted the palomino and turned him toward the trail back to the river. For a moment, hoofbeats on the soft ground were the only sound. "Hey, maybe there's another hermit living out here," she suggested. "And he shot his gun into the air to scare off the searchers."

Jani laughed. "Yeah, like there are a bunch of hermits out here."

"It's possible. There could be an entire population of hermits. It could be like Hermit-ville or something, and no one would ever know it exists."

"Not even the hermits," said Jani, warming to the idea. "Because that's what hermits do; they hide all the time."

"And after he shot into the air, your mom chased him away on Champagne."

The two girls grinned at each other – Jani's mom chasing anyone was ridiculous, especially while riding a horse, even one as well trained as Champagne. Jani's smile disappeared when she thought of why her mom was out on

Champagne in the first place. "What should we do now?" she asked. "Hailey might still be at Joe's house."

A sudden icy rain pummeled them. Penny screamed and reached back to wrestle her already wet hoodie over her head.

"Over here," cried Jani, directing Keeta to the nearest large tree. She asked the mare to sidestep nearer the trunk. Freedom followed her, her ears pinned back and head lowered beneath the cold deluge. Sunny looked totally miserable as he and Penny joined them beneath the tree.

"I'm so sick of rain, I could scream," said Penny.

"You did scream."

"Ha ha, so funny."

"At least we're soaked all over now. Dad won't know we were running across wet fields to look through windows." Cold rain spilled through the thick boughs. Jani sighed. If only they'd seen Hailey at Joe's. At least they would've known she was alive. At least she'd have shelter from this freezing rain. "Poor Hailey," she said.

"I know. I wish she'd been there."

"Maybe we just didn't see her."

"Maybe." Penny sounded doubtful.

"Jani!"

"Dad! Over here!" Jani waved.

Her dad and Apollo looked as if they'd taken a swim in the river, they were so wet. "Did you hear the flare?"

Jani raised her eyebrows. The signal flare. How could they have forgotten? The sound wasn't a rifle shot at all, and here they were making up silly stories – no wonder her dad didn't take her suspicions about Joe seriously. Aloud she said, "Yeah, we heard it."

"I'm hoping it means they found her. Let's hurry back to the meeting place at the bridge."

HAILEY

Could her grandfather *not* be her grandfather? Could he be a stranger who was lying to her? Was that why she couldn't remember him? Was that why he'd been reluctant to say her name in the woods and why the name seemed so unfamiliar once he'd said it?

Unbidden, the flash of blue she'd seen under the window leapt into her mind. The cupful of water almost slipped from her grasp. If a stranger was keeping her captive, there was only one reason for someone to hide under the window. Someone knew she was there. Someone may want to rescue her! Maybe the man whose voice she'd heard while waking from her dream, the man her "grandfather" was worried she'd overheard! It all made sense now!

With her heart thudding in her ears, she rushed to the window – to see the man who claimed to be her grandfather striding toward the front door, the only exit she'd seen from the cabin!

Water splashed from the cup as she spun around. Maybe she could get through a window. Maybe…

Dizziness struck again, descending like a dark fog, dulling her senses. She reached out to grab something, anything, that might stop her from falling. She couldn't faint now. She would be at his mercy then – unless she somehow got back to the bedroom first. She fell to her knees and the cup clattered to the floor, spilling the last of its contents. Using all her strength, she crawled toward the bedroom. She wasn't going to make it out of the cabin, but if she could just lock the bedroom door maybe she'd be safe until help came.

If it came.

If the person on the other side of the window was looking for her.

If they had seen her.

She felt like throwing up. She'd thought about opening the curtain to see the photo. If she had, the person outside would have known for sure she was there.

But maybe they'd seen her move through the thick material. Maybe there had been a crack between the curtains and the edge of the window. She couldn't give up yet.

Somehow she made it into the bedroom. She pushed the door closed just as the man opened the front door. Now to lock it. Then she could give in to the dizziness. Then she could collapse.

His footfalls were coming closer to the door.

And there was no lock!

"Jenny?" His deep voice came through the wood.

"Don't come in!"

"I won't. I just want to tell you, in case you're worried, that noise? It meant nothing."

"What noise?" She pushed her back against the door. She knew it wouldn't stop him, but she had to do something to protect herself.

"That gunshot. It was nothing, okay? Just a distant hunter or maybe someone target practicing. I don't want you to worry."

"O...okay," the girl said, trying to sound calmer. Obviously, he didn't realize she knew about his lie yet.

"I'm still tired, Gram…" She couldn't finish the word. It seemed so wrong to call him Grandpa.

"Are you sure you're okay?" Now he sounded concerned. Somehow she had to get him away from her door. "Do you want a drink or something to eat?"

"I'm fine," she said, as firmly as she could. *Except I feel like throwing up, can't even stand because I'm so dizzy, and am scared half to death. I'm just fine.* She pressed her hands to her face. Her skin felt too hot.

"Okay. Well, I'll come check on you again in a little while. I'm almost finished with the truck. Then we can go, alright?"

"Okay."

There was a long silence, and then finally, *finally,* she heard the sound of booted feet moving away from her door. The front door banged shut.

The girl sighed. She'd been given a reprieve. Fighting the dizziness the whole time, she moved to the chair beside the dresser. Slowly, determinedly, she scooted it toward the door, not caring how much noise it made as it scraped across the floor. The man was outside now. He wouldn't hear.

When she finally had it by the bedroom door, she tipped the chair backwards, fit its back under the doorknob, and pushed it snug.

There. He couldn't get in now unless he knocked the entire door down.

She crawled back to the window and reached up to tug the curtain aside. Her rescuers needed to see her if they came to her window again. She made her way to the bed and somehow found the strength to climb up into its softness and cuddle into the blankets. Then finally she allowed the alluring darkness to claim her.

JANI

They were the first group back to the river, but another showed up within a couple of minutes. They hadn't seen Hailey either, and the mood was quiet and tense as the six riders waited under the trees near the bridge. Rain continued to fall, swift and icy cold.

The rest of the riders arrived about ten minutes later.

"Mom, did you find her?" Jani yelled as she galloped Keeta through the wet to greet them. Mud sprayed around them as Keeta slid to a stop.

Her mom shook her head. "We have to call the search off. Carl's satellite radio says there's worse weather on the way, a lot more rain and possibly sleet and snow. We can't risk anything happening to any of the amateur searchers. But don't worry," she continued, seeing the dismayed expression on Jani's face. "The professional Search and Rescue teams will still be out and they'll probably recruit some people with wilderness experience, like your dad."

"What about me? I'm an experienced rider." Jani reined Keeta to walk beside her mom's beautiful cremello mount.

Jani's mom shook her head. "I don't want you out in this."

"But Mom –"

"I know it's hard to sit home and wait, Jani, but you can't help when the conditions are dangerous. If something happened to you, it would do more than completely break my heart – it would slow the search for Hailey."

"But nothing's going to happen to me."

"Elaine's horse almost slid into the river already, when the bank gave way right beside them, and with more rain, the ground will become softer and the river higher. It'll be going over the bank in a lot more places."

"But what about Hailey? She's out here. She needs us."

"I know. And it makes me sick to think about it, especially when she needs her insulin." Jani's mom looked like she was about to cry.

"What do you mean? What's insulin?"

"Hailey's diabetic. I thought you knew. She needs insulin, or, well, eventually she'll go into a coma."

Jani pulled Keeta to a stop. Hailey had a disease? How had she never heard? Even if the girl survived the car wreck and the trip down the river, she still had something that might kill her if they didn't find her in time. How could they all just go home? How could they abandon her?

But her mom wasn't going to relent, she knew that for certain. She'd already done all she was allowed to do.

Elaine stopped Rain Shadow beside her. "Jani, I'm sorry."

Jani had to look up at the younger girl because Rain Shadow was so tall. "Sorry for what?" she asked, surprised.

"I was mad at you last night," said Elaine, looking down at her reins. "Hailey told me she was going to your house today instead of riding with me, and I was… well, I was jealous, I guess."

"She wasn't coming over because she likes me more than you. I was just helping her with something."

"What?"

"I can't say. I promised her I'd keep it a secret," Jani said reluctantly.

Elaine looked crestfallen.

"But I can tell you one thing," Jani added. "The thing she was doing? It was for you."

Elaine wiped rainwater and tears from her face. "Do you think we'll find her? Before it's too late?"

Jani didn't know what to say. She'd asked others that question, but no one had asked her. Did she think they'd find Hailey alive? Logic said no, especially now that she knew about Hailey's condition. But on the other hand there was Freedom and her strange antics. *Something* had happened between Freedom and Joe, and the only possible connection between the two was Hailey.

"Do you?" Elaine asked again, her voice small and vulnerable.

Jani nodded. "Yeah, I do." And she meant it.

FREEDOM

The barn was cozy and warm and her dam seemed content. The manger was filled with hay and the grain bin had a few tasty morsels lingering at the bottom. Fresh water waited in the bucket. The rain pounding the roof of the barn made her grateful she wasn't out in the horrendous weather – and yet, all she could do was pace.

A showdown was coming between her and Monster Man, this one that Jani called Joe. She could feel it in her blood, in her bones. Would she be able to free Hailey? Would she even be able to save herself? This time, would she be strong enough?

She wasn't the last time.

Keeta nickered and nuzzled her daughter, but Freedom hardly noticed. She walked past her dam, turned, and walked past her again. Keeta whinnied again. Finally, unwilling to be ignored any longer, Keeta bunted Freedom with her nose. The filly stopped to stare at her. Why was her dam so intent on making her rest, or eat, or do other trivial things?

But Keeta didn't encourage Freedom to lie down and rest. She didn't motion to her daughter to eat the last of the grain. Instead, she nuzzled her with a concerned look in her eyes and Freedom understood. Her dam was worried about the girl too; she wanted to help.

For the first time since seeing Monster Man, Freedom relaxed. This time was different than when she'd last faced him and his horrible partner. She was no longer alone. Keeta was with her – and Jani too, if she could just get her human to understand. With them beside her, she could – and would – face Monster Man.

But would it be enough to save Hailey?

HAILEY

"Jenny!" There was a loud knocking and then the strange name came again. "Jenny!"

The girl woke to a lightless room.

"Go away." Was that her voice? It was so wimpy. She reached out to switch on a light, though she didn't remember if there was a lamp by the bed or not.

"Jenny? Can you hear me?"

There was no lamp and suddenly, the girl realized what the darkness meant. It was night. Tears pricked her eyes. No one had come. What was she going to do? She pulled the covers up closer to her chin and burrowed down in the blankets.

"Jenny, the truck is fixed. I can take you to the hospital now."

"I want to sleep."

"Are you okay?"

"I'm fine. Just tired," she said, trying to sound stronger. If she was going to get out of this situation, she was going to have to make him think she wasn't weak and sick and exhausted.

The doorknob rattled. "You have to at least eat something."

"I'm not hungry."

"Dinner's almost ready. I'll be back when it's finished. You have to unlock the door then, okay?" He didn't wait for her response before moving heavily away.

"I'm never going to open it," the girl whispered. "Not to you." She shut her eyes. What was she going to do? At least, she felt a bit better after her rest – not quite so dizzy, though she was still terribly thirsty and the rain thundering on the roof made her even more that way. If she opened the window, she could get something to drink without letting the man in, and maybe she could even slip out and run away.

Gradually, she pushed herself up, but the higher she got, the dizzier she became. She felt burning hot and freezing cold at the same time. She fell back. She was still too weak. More rest, that's what she needed, even more than she needed a drink. There would be time later, in the middle of the night when her captor was asleep, to run away.

JANI

Jani leaned back in her bedroom's window seat, her eyes unfocussed and her thoughts far away. The more she thought about the events that afternoon, the more convinced she was that Joe knew something about Hailey's disappearance. There was no other reason for Freedom to go to his cabin, no other explanation for the way she acted when she saw the man. And who kept their curtains tightly drawn in the middle of the day when they had no neighbors to peer inside? No one, unless they had something to hide.

Jani sighed and closed her eyes. And yet there was nothing – no clues or evidence – that anyone else would take seriously. Her dad had already told her, before rushing off to continue helping with the search, to quit talking about poor old Joe. He wasn't a bad guy, just a fellow who liked his privacy and wasn't used to people.

Jani tried to convince her mom after he left and Penny had talked to her parents too, but no one really listened. They were all convinced that Joe wouldn't hurt a fly.

"Brown Bear, what are we going to do?" she said aloud to her ancient teddy bear. Talking out her problems with the bear was a habit she'd never been able to break, not that she'd tried that hard. Talking to Brown Bear sometimes helped her figure things out, though she knew it had nothing to do with her beloved teddy. It was the act of speaking her thoughts aloud that helped her focus.

"No one believes us. We have to convince them somehow, but how? We need proof." Jani gasped. "Proof." She jumped up from the window seat, then rushed to her bed and hugged the scruffy bear lounging on her covers. "I know just what to do. You're awesome." Brown Bear stared back at her with his one eye, a know-it-all smile on his cute, satisfied face.

She ran downstairs and hurried to the phone in the kitchen. When Penny picked up at her end, Jani didn't waste time with hellos.

"I know what we can do," she blurted. "See if you're allowed out for a couple of hours, okay? We're going to the newspaper office to find dirt on Joe."

Half an hour later, Jani, Penny, and Jani's mom arrived at the newspaper office owned by Jani's parents. "I don't know what you girls think you're going to find in the archives," she said.

"We thought we'd look up some information about past floods," said Jani, hoping her mom wouldn't ask any more questions. She didn't want to actually lie to her, and in a way, their true purpose did have *something* to do with floods. Kind of.

"Well, good luck. The archives are a mess. We really need to get them catalogued and properly protected," her mom replied. She pointed toward the far wall where stacks of newspapers were sitting on shelves. "The oldest ones are on the left. If you feel like double checking that they're in the right order as you go through them, feel free."

Jani turned her head so her mom wouldn't see her grimace, but she needn't have bothered. Her mom was already turning toward the main office. Searching for Hailey had taken priority over everything all day, but that didn't mean there wasn't tons of work to do if they were going to get the weekly Red River Report newspaper out on time.

"Thanks, Mrs. Preston," Penny said to the retreating back. "What a great idea, Jani," she said as soon as Jani's mom disappeared into her office. "If there's any information on Joe that'll prove he's a bad guy, we'll find it here."

"I hope so. Otherwise, no one will ever believe us enough to search his cabin." She picked up the oldest pile of archive newspapers, carried them to a table, then checked the date of the paper on top. "How old do you think Joe is?"

"Seventy maybe? Or more?"

Jani sighed as she took the paper off the top of the pile. "So I guess we start with the oldest papers. He would've been in his twenties then." She bent over the old print and scanned the headlines.

Penny took the next paper off the pile. "At least they didn't have a lot of news back then. This one is only four pages long," she said as she started to skim.

"What's Joe's last name, by the way?"

Penny thought for a moment. "Mason, I think."

"You think?"

"I'm pretty sure."

By the time they were halfway through the pile, the length of the newspapers didn't seem so important – all it meant was there were more newspapers in the pile. By the time they reached the bottom of the first stack, an hour had passed and Jani felt a headache coming on. Twenty years of Red River history had passed before her eyes, most of it boring, but the interesting stuff was incredibly interesting. She'd had no idea that in the late sixties, the river had gotten so high that half the town had to be evacuated. She read of how when one young boy was carried from his home by a fireman, he was crying. The fireman asked him what was wrong and he said his puppy was still in the house, so the fireman went back for it, only to find it swimming in the basement, close to exhaustion. He saved the puppy and the boy was happy. Jani found herself smiling as she read – it was nice to read a happy flood story. Everything else was about homes damaged by the high water and precious items lost or destroyed forever.

She shuddered as she thought of how dangerous the river looked that very afternoon. Hopefully, it wasn't going to keep getting higher, as it did in the sixties, but with all this rain, how could it not?

Silently, she moved the first stack back onto the shelf and brought the second stack to the table. Penny stretched before starting to read again, then they both dove back into skimming headlines and articles. The individual papers were getting longer by the edition. Red River was becoming more populated and there was more news. There was no need to read the Sports and Entertainment section though, or the Classified Ads.

They were only three newspapers down in the second pile, when another name jumped up at Jani from the front page – Hansen. Quickly, she skimmed the article. Yes, this was the Mr. Hansen who had trapped Freedom in a barn when she was a wild mustang. This was the Mr. Hansen who had caused her death because he refused to set her free when she wouldn't be tamed. Jani was positive it was him because it told of his riding accident when he became paralyzed. Of course, it wouldn't mention the part that Freedom played in his accident – she'd been a ghost then.

She gasped when she reached the bottom of the article. "Oh wow," she said, almost speechless.

"What?"

"You have to read this, Penny."

As Penny took the article and started to read, Jani stared into space. This article wasn't good news. It gave Freedom another motive for being afraid of Joe, which meant that her fear of him might have nothing to do with Hailey's disappearance. Unfortunately, Freedom's odd behavior may have its roots in the past.

HAILEY

True to his word, the man pretending to be her grandfather was back minutes later.

"Jenny, open this door." He sounded firmer this time. "It's time to eat, and then we're leaving."

"No," she whispered, then wondered if she'd said it loud enough for him to hear. But it didn't matter. He'd get the idea soon enough when she didn't open the door.

There was a long silence, then the sound of a throat clearing. "I… I found the water and cup on the floor. You saw the photos on the mantle, didn't you? You know the truth."

The girl swallowed nervously. What would he do if she confessed? Get angry? Break down the door? But she couldn't say she still believed he was her grandfather when she didn't – and if she remained silent, he'd guess anyway. "Yes, I know."

"I only said it because you looked so confused and frightened in the forest. That's the only reason. Now open the door. I can bring in a lantern for you, so you're not sitting in the dark, and you can have some supper."

"My name isn't Jenny, is it?" she asked, forcing herself to sit up in the bed. Bright lights flashed in the darkness and she felt the room spinning. "You don't know my name, do you?"

"No, I'm sorry," he said. There was a long pause. "Jenny was my daughter."

She fought back another wave of dizziness. "Was?" she asked. "What do you mean, *was* your daughter?"

"She…well…" He cleared his throat. "That has nothing to do with you needing food," the man said firmly. "And I know you say you feel fine, but sometimes feelings can be wrong. You really should see a doctor. They can help you find your family too." When she didn't answer, he continued, his voice more gentle, "And you can't stay in there forever. You need to eat. Even if you're not sick, you don't want to get that way by being stubborn."

Maybe that was why she was feeling so weak. Maybe that was why resting wasn't helping. She must need food. She hadn't eaten all day. But she couldn't open the door. She'd be at his mercy then.

"What if I leave the food by the door, and go outside where you can see me through the window? Then you can open your door and bring the food back into your room to eat."

"If I do that, will you leave me alone? Let me rest?"

"Okay," he said, reluctantly. "But you have to promise me that you really do feel fine."

"I'm just…" she stopped. She was going to repeat that she was tired, but thought better of it. This stranger might say that was enough reason to take her to the hospital. "I'm just fine," she said, then added, "I need some more water too."

"Alright."

She heard him move away from the door and come back, then the scrape of a plate against the floor, and finally, silence.

"Now go outside the window, where I can see you." The words felt like molasses pouring from her mouth, thick and heavy.

When she heard the faint sound of the door to the outside shutting, she slowly pushed herself to a standing position and lurched toward the window.

What was wrong with her? She was feeling worse, not better, after her rests. Maybe she *should* trust him to take her to the hospital.

Her hands shook as she gripped the windowsill. There he was, standing a few yards away, holding a lantern. Rain was gusting against his body and he already looked soaked through.

She pulled the curtain across the window so he couldn't see her and stumbled toward the door. It was a major endeavor just to get that far and when she arrived, she leaned against it, breathing hard.

Dare she open the door? If she had taken too long to cross the room, he could be outside the door, waiting for her. She turned and stared back at the curtains. She had to know if he was still out there, but the window seemed farther away than ever.

She slumped to the floor. If only she could give up. But if she left the dinner outside, he'd know there was something wrong with her. If she wanted him to keep his promise to leave her alone, she had to bring the plate into the room.

With every passing second he was more likely to be outside that door – if he wasn't there already.

Somehow she pushed the chair out of the way and reached for the doorknob, then scooted out of the way so the door could open a crack. He wasn't there! As quickly as she could, she snagged the edge of the tray holding the plate, cup of water, and a flashlight. With weak fingers, she slid it toward herself. The water slopped onto the food, but she didn't care. She just had to get it out of his sight.

She heard the front door open and looked up, wild-eyed.

He was coming!

She shoved the door shut moments later and struggled to put the chair back under the doorknob. It was so ungainly, so hard to maneuver.

"You don't need to do that," his voice came from the other side of the door, making her jump. "I'm not going to hurt you."

"I'm sorry," she whispered, and for a moment she was. But then her reason returned – this was a stranger, a stranger who had already lied to her. She couldn't trust him. Finally, she got the back of the chair under the doorknob and tried to push it snug, then felt for the flashlight and clicked it on.

"In the morning, I'll drive into town and tell the police you're here."

She curled up on the rough wood floor. Why didn't her captor just go away?

"Do you like your dinner?"

She stared at the food. It looked so unappetizing. But she'd eat it. She'd make herself both eat and drink. "It's okay," she lied.

"Well, if you need anything, just call me. I'll be in the next room."

The girl didn't bother responding. Instead, she pulled her knees closer to her chest. She'd stick to her plan: as soon as she had another rest, she'd force herself to eat and then she'd run away.

JANI

"Mom?"

Jani's mom turned toward them and Jani noticed the dark circles under her eyes. After the long day of searching and now all this office work, she was obviously tired.

"You girls about ready to call it a night?" she asked. "I know I am." She rose to her feet and pulled her jacket off the back of her chair.

"We found something for you to read," said Jani. She thrust the old newspaper forward.

Her mom slipped on her jacket, sighed, and sat down again. "Which article?"

"The one about the missing girl."

Jani's mom scanned the article – the second one that Jani and Penny had found that mentioned Joe Mason. Unfortunately they couldn't show her the first one, the one that had made the most impact on them, because her mom didn't know the story of Freedom's birth. It would mean nothing to her that Joe and Mr. Hansen had been partners in the past, right before Mr. Hansen's accident. The fact that they'd caught mustangs together would be completely meaningless, because there was no way she'd believe that Freedom had been one of those mustangs, let alone that she'd died because of Mr. Hansen's cruelty – and possibly Joe's too.

However, this second article, it would mean something

to her. She might even find it important enough to get the authorities to search Joe's cabin.

"Did you read about what happened next?" Jani's mom asked, looking up from the article with a worried expression. "There would be a follow-up story about something this important."

"We thought we should let you read it right away."

"Well, let's check the next few issues."

The girls followed her back to the pile of archive newspapers. She skimmed through the headlines of the next edition, while Jani and Penny tackled the two after. It didn't take long to find out what happened.

"Here it is," said Penny.

Jani looked up to see disappointment on Penny's face. "What?"

"She went to live at her aunt's house."

"But wouldn't her dad know she was going there?"

"Maybe she ran away," Penny said hopefully.

Jani's mom took the paper and read the rest of the article. "She did run away, but not because of anything her dad did. It says she wanted to live in town with her aunt. She must have missed her mom." Jani's mom put the newspaper down. "The newspaper says her mother died the year before."

Jani sat back and closed her eyes. And they'd been so close to proving that Joe was a suspicious character. For a moment she thought of telling her mom the story of Freedom's past, but dismissed the idea just as quickly. Her mom wouldn't believe it and then she'd be even more reluctant to investigate Joe, thinking Jani was being unreasonable and, well… crazy.

She sighed. What more could they do? No one believed them that Hailey might be at Joe's house. In fact, she wasn't even sure herself anymore, after reading the article about Joe and Freedom's mutual past.

"You ready, girls?" asked Jani's mom.

"Yeah," Jani said quietly.

Her mom put her hand on Jani's shoulder. "Try not to be discouraged, honey. There's still hope."

"Yeah," she said again, even quieter.

Penny elbowed her in the side and when Jani looked at her, she covered an exaggerated yawn with her hand. Then she winked.

A small smile appeared on Jani's face despite herself. Penny was so great.

"What's wrong, Pen? Tired?"

"Exhausted."

"Me too," said Jani's mom, but she sounded like she meant it.

"I'm going to bed as soon as I get home," said Penny as they moved toward the door.

"And maybe we'll have good news about Hailey in the morning," added Jani, catching on immediately.

"That's the spirit, girls." Once outside, Jani's mom turned to lock the door.

Jani smiled at Penny. They would go to bed soon and they might have good news for everyone by morning – for as soon as their parents were asleep, they would go search for Hailey.

It was possible that Freedom's reaction to Joe had been all about their shared past. Maybe the filly wasn't trying to tell Jani that Hailey was there. Maybe they were accusing some innocent guy for nothing. But it didn't matter. She and Penny had to go back to Joe's house. They had to find the truth, whatever it was, and if no one would help them? Well, then they'd do it themselves.

FREEDOM

At last, Jani must understand. Freedom waited impatiently as her girl silently saddled Keeta.

Why had she doubted that her human was smart enough to put it all together? Jani might be a bit slow figuring things out sometimes, but she always came through.

When Jani came toward her with the foal halter in her hands, she ducked around to the other side of her dam.

"Come on, Freedom. You have to have a rope on. It's too dangerous out there," Jani murmured as she followed. "It's stormy and windy, and the middle of the night."

Freedom snorted and backed up. She really didn't like being contained in any way, but she'd always allowed it because she trusted Jani. But to be held by ropes when she was near Monster Man? The thought made her heart race and her muscles shudder. If Monster Man got hold of her rope… well, who knew what he'd do?

But what if Jani wouldn't leave until she wore the rope? She turned and stared through the small window into the night. Hailey's need was calling her.

Suddenly, the rope was around her neck. She reared up, automatically striking out in fear, and Jani cried out and fell back. Keeta leapt between them, her ears pinned.

Why did you do that? You knew the life you chose when you came back!

Her front legs came to the ground, trembling. She'd struck at Jani, the one she loved – and why? Was she still

so afraid of the past? The man couldn't hurt her anymore. Jani and Keeta wouldn't let him. Hadn't she already decided that?

"Freedom?" Jani's voice shook as she climbed to her feet.

The foal nickered, nuzzled Keeta on the neck, and slipped around her toward her girl. Approaching slowly, she whinnied apologetically to Jani.

Jani let the rope fall to the ground. "I'm sorry, Freedom," she whispered and held out her hand.

The filly nuzzled it, then stepped closer to her girl and pressed her forehead against Jani's chest. This girl was her heart. This girl was her life. If only there was some way she could make up for scaring her, for striking out at her in her surprise and panic.

With resolve, she picked up the lead rope that Jani had dropped. If her girl wanted her to wear her halter and lead rope, she would. Keeta was right. She'd chosen this path when she returned to live with the girl she loved. She was a mustang no longer. It was time to leave the past behind.

JANI

Within moments of leaving the barn, Jani and the two horses were soaked. The wind was gusting so hard that the rain streamed sideways. Even Jani's slicker couldn't keep out the wet. It pummeled her face under her hood and slid cold, unwelcome fingers down her neck. Freedom and Keeta lowered their heads beneath the deluge.

Penny waited for her at the end of Solomon Way. In the beam of Jani's flashlight, she and Sunny looked absolutely dejected.

"Great night, huh?" said Jani and clicked off the light.

"Lovely," Penny said as the two started down the road. They needed to travel about a mile along the main road, then turn onto a side road that eventually branched onto the logging road that led to the bridge where the search party had met that afternoon. Then, somehow, they needed to find Joe's driveway in the dark, when all it would be was a rough, narrow track off of a logging road. If worst came to worst though, they could always follow the path they'd ridden that afternoon – along the swollen river, then through the forest, and onto the road near his house – but Jani sincerely hoped they didn't have to do that. It had been dangerous enough riding along the flooding river that afternoon, but in the dark? It could be suicidal.

"Good thing we're the only crazy ones out tonight," Penny said above the pounding of the rain. "Otherwise someone might see us and tell our parents."

Jani laughed, but it sounded forced. What *were* they doing out here, riding through the night? Even if they found Joe's place in this terrible darkness and Hailey was there, what could they do to rescue her? They were just two kids.

"I think Mom suspected something tonight," Penny continued. "Her light was on until almost 1 o'clock."

"Not my parents," said Jani. "They were in bed by eleven and asleep two minutes later. I heard Dad snoring. He sounded like a grizzly bear, growling over and over and over."

"Amazing your mom can sleep through that."

"She has earplugs." As they turned onto the side road, Jani sighed. Still so far to go.

One step at a time, that's how we do this, Jani reminded herself. *And the next step is to find where the old logging road branches off.*

It wasn't as hard as Jani thought it would be. The road was well traveled, because even though no one but Joe lived back there, lots of people fished in the river and the hikers enjoyed the riverside trails.

Jani pulled Freedom to Keeta's side and bent to unfasten the lead rope from her halter. There would be no traffic on the road at this time of night. Freedom was safe to trot at liberty alongside her dam and Sunny.

The old logging road gained steadily in elevation for some time. Freedom loped ahead, then trotted reluctantly back, as if trying to encourage them to go faster. Keeta and Sunny ignored her hints and kept to a steady jog.

Jani could tell her mare was tired. She reached to pat the warm shoulder, slick with sweat and rain. When the road descended into a side valley, the two older horses moved faster.

Jani felt pleased. They were close to the bridge now. They'd made good time and most importantly, they'd remained completely unobserved. What more could they ask?

Okay, maybe for a little less rain.

"I hear the river," Penny said.

"Me too."

A scuffling sound came from the road ahead, then the rattle of gravel followed by a huge sploosh. With her heart thudding like mad, Jani clicked on her flashlight and pointed it toward the strange noise.

The road in front of them was gone, washed away by a raging side channel that hadn't been there that afternoon. The flooding river had overflowed its banks, creating new streams and smaller rivers, one of which had taken out the road! Jani moved the flashlight beam farther out into the churning water and her heart squeezed painfully. A small black form struggled against the furious current.

"Freedom!" Jani screamed.

Keeta leapt forward. The mare didn't hesitate at the water's edge, but plunged into the swift running flow, throwing Jani forward onto her neck. When Keeta lunged forward in an effort to regain her footing, Jani clung to the long mane with all her strength. Dirty, freezing water splashed them both, soaking the last dry spots beneath her slicker.

When Keeta finally stood firm, Jani regained her balance and directed her toward the struggling black filly. Though Freedom was big enough – barely – to keep her hooves on the ground, the current was slowly and relentlessly pushing her toward deeper water. Very soon, she would be swimming and shortly after that, she'd be in the main channel of the river, buffeted by logs and other debris.

Just like Hailey…

Jani shoved the thought from her head. "Hurry, Keeta, hurry," she murmured as they pushed toward the foal. Amazingly, Freedom wasn't panicking, or not yet anyway. Instead, she was straining toward the far bank, slowly, steadily, and methodically. Her elegant head, neck, and back were all that was visible above the raging water.

Jani heard another sploosh behind her, and knew that Penny and Sunny had entered the washout but she didn't dare tear her eyes from Freedom. What if that was the moment that the current picked her up and swept her away? Slowly, she and Keeta gained on the little horse, then they were behind her, and finally beside her on the downstream side.

The swift running water shoved Freedom against Keeta's side, but the mare didn't falter. She was stronger than this current now that she'd found her balance. She kept straight on to the opposite bank, her foal plastered to her side.

Jani risked a quick look back. Sunny and Penny were right behind them – and did Sunny ever look upset. His ears were back and his head jutted forward. He looked like all he wanted to do was turn around and run back to his warm, dry stall. Penny was leaning over his neck encouraging him on, stroking his well-muscled shoulder.

When they reached the far shore, Freedom tried to scramble up the bank. On her first attempt, she slid back into the water, but on her second try, Keeta pushed her hard with her head, boosting her up.

Moments later, they were all standing on the road, shivering and dripping. Penny stripped off her useless mittens and wrung them out. “Well,” she said in a fake British accent, “that was quite the adventure.”

“Yes, quite.” Jani smiled.

“Shall we sally forth?”

“Why, yes. What a perfectly splendid idea.”

HAILEY

She was only half aware of the shouting. It seemed so far away, so removed from her and her situation. She tried once to hear what the voice was saying but it just kept yelling some strange name, so she allowed herself to slip back into the fog.

A loud crash jolted her out of her repose. A form moved over her, its movement quick with… what? Anger? Fear? She closed her eyes. She was too tired to figure it out. She'd think about it later.

But then the person picked her up in shaking arms.

"What're you doing?"

"Nothing. Just lie still." A man's voice said.

"Leave me alone. Where's my mom?" Her mom would make him put her down. She'd force him to let her sleep.

"You remember your mother?"

Why would he ask such a stupid thing? Was he crazy? Of course she remembered her mother. Didn't she? Only… she couldn't remember what she looked like. Or her name. Cold fear crawled over her body.

And suddenly, the day's memories came back to her. She'd been found on the edge of the river by a man who claimed to be her grandfather, but who was really lying to her. He wasn't family or friend. He was a stranger.

Dreading the worst, she turned her head to see the face of whoever was holding her. She was in the arms of the old guy who had lied to her! He'd broken down the door to her safe sanctuary and carried her out!

She came alive – kicking, hitting, thrashing, screaming – anything to get away from this stranger.

The man groaned when her fist made contact with his eye, but he didn't drop her. Instead, he gently lowered her to a couch, then started to wrap a blanket around her. Cocooning her. Pinning her arms to her side.

What was he going to do with her? She had to get away, but she could hardly move. He was bundling her up, just like a big baby. She had to do something – anything – before it was too late.

JANI

A minute later, they reached the bridge that crossed the main part of the river. As usual, Freedom was ahead of them.

"Careful, Freedom," Jani called, keeping her flashlight's beam on the black horse. As if she'd understood Jani's warning, the filly stopped, then lowered her head to sniff at the planks surfacing the bridge.

Jani pulled Keeta to a stop beside Freedom and the light from her flashlight danced across the boards. "It's shaking. The bridge is shaking," she said in amazement. "Look at that, Penny."

"Do you think it's safe to cross?"

"The horses will know. We'll let them decide."

The horses stood, their rain-soaked heads slumped morosely for a full minute before one of them moved – and of course the first to step forward was Freedom. She walked cautiously onto the bridge, stood still for a long moment, then strode across. Seconds later, Keeta followed her and then Sunny. The thud of their hooves on the wood was lost to the roar of the river and it felt odd to feel the vibrations of the bridge come right up Keeta's legs.

"I'm amazed they'd cross, even if it is safe," Penny shouted behind her.

"I don't know if they would have if Freedom hadn't gone first," Jani answered, watching the filly walking before them.

They were almost across the bridge when Freedom stopped short.

"What's wrong?" yelled Penny. "Don't stop here."

Light flashed through the rain – headlights coming from the other side of the bridge!

"Someone's coming!" Jani yelled. She urged Keeta into a gallop and they raced over the rest of the expanse, passing Freedom where the bridge met the road. "Come on, Freedom," Jani called to the filly and directed Keeta toward the trees they'd stood beneath that afternoon. Once they were in the forest, whoever was in the approaching vehicle wouldn't see them. They'd be safe from discovery.

She pulled the pinto to a halt beneath the boughs and Penny and Sunny came to a panting stop beside her.

"Who is it? Can you tell?" asked Penny, staring toward the approaching headlights.

"No. I just hope our parents didn't notice we're gone."

"It can't be them. Whoever it is, they're coming from the wrong side of the bridge."

"Maybe it's Joe," Jani whispered. The vehicle was almost alongside them now. Was it Joe's old truck?

It was!

Suddenly, the driver slammed on the brakes. The vehicle slid sideways, sending a wake of water and mud flying around it. Jani thought she heard a scream, but she had to be mistaken…

He'd seen them. Somehow, he'd seen them.

Then her heart seemed to freeze. It wasn't her, Penny, or the two adult horses that had made Joe brake.

Directly between the truck and the bridge, with her eyes blazing, ears pinned back, hooves stamping, and tail switching, stood Freedom!

HAILEY

The girl flew forward and a scream burst from her mouth. Her shoulder hit something, hard. Where was she? What was happening? She felt so cold, so distant from everything. Even the pain in her shoulder seemed far away.

"No, not her! She can't be here," said a panicked, grown-up voice.

A man was with her – and he sounded terrified. Then a strong, rough hand was moving her, picking her up by her unhurt arm, scooting her back.

When he let her go, the girl summoned enough energy to turn her head and open her eyes. What had she struck? The dashboard of a truck. And who was the man who helped her back to the seat?

"I'm sorry, are you okay?" he said.

She could barely see him in the faint glow from the dashboard lights. Should she know him? She didn't think so. "What happened?" she whispered.

"It's her." The man stared out the windshield again, his face white and wan. "She's come back."

Slowly, with great effort, the girl raised up just enough to look out the truck windshield. There was a black foal on the road.

And she knew this baby horse. She'd seen her before.

"Freedom," she murmured and smiled. Jani, Freedom's owner, was going to teach her to like horses, so that someone – who? – would never know she was afraid of them. *Elaine*, that's who. She couldn't let Elaine know she was afraid, not ever, because Elaine loved horses.

"What did you say?"

"Freedom," Hailey whispered.

"How can you know her name?" The stranger sounded like he was choking on his own words.

"I remember her. And I remember…" Hailey gasped and her eyes opened wide. She remembered the car careening across a road in the rain. The river coming up to crash into the windshield. Her mom not answering her cries. Undoing her own seatbelt so she could run to get help – and the river, the cold, cruel river, sweeping her away. Then she'd awakened on the riverbank, and was found by this man who pretended to be her grandfather, who held her prisoner.

"Tell me how you know that horse," the man said. He leaned toward her to hear her better. "What's she doing here? How did she come back? I don't understand."

Hailey tried to tell him to get away from her, but her mouth wouldn't open. Her tongue was too thick to move.

She closed her eyes. She couldn't take any more. What if her mom was dead? Everything was too horrible, too scary. More than anything, she wanted to sink down into the darkness, away from her terror, away from her exhaustion, away from her illness and aloneness and pain.

And she did.

FREEDOM

Freedom's legs trembled as the vehicle raced toward her. When it slid to a halt, stopping inches in front of her, it took all her strength and courage not to run away. Monster Man was inside that truck. He might capture her again, take her away from her home.

Hailey was in the truck too, though she couldn't see her chestnut hair above the dashboard. However, she could feel the girl's presence, weak though it was. She could feel Hailey's need. Had Monster Man hurt her?

Freedom snorted. Whatever Monster Man had done to the girl, he could do to her too – but she would face him, no matter the cost. She had to stop him from taking the girl away.

JANI

"What do we do now?" whispered Penny.

"I bet Hailey's in there."

Penny's forehead creased as she looked at the truck. "I don't see her."

Jani slid from Keeta's back and quickly tied the mare's reins to a tree branch. "We wouldn't though. It's too dark in the truck, and besides, she might be lying on the seat. We need to get her out of there without Joe seeing."

"Oh, is that all? Any ideas on how to do the impossible?" Penny was on the ground now too, tying Sunny securely beside Keeta.

The interior lights abruptly dissolved the darkness inside the truck when the driver's door opened. Joe was going after Freedom! Jani watched helpless as he left the door hanging ajar and walked cautiously toward the filly. Surely Freedom wouldn't let the man get a hold of her.

"See? She's not in there," said Penny.

Jani hardly heard her. Her filly was letting Joe get far too close – then suddenly, Freedom bobbed her head and backed a few paces, her blue eyes bright in the headlights. "We have to look inside," said Jani, relieved. "Let's go." This might be the only time they'd have to save Hailey, if she was even in the truck.

She and Penny raced toward the old vehicle, bent low, just in case Joe heard the sound of their wet feet slapping through the puddles and turned to look. Finally, they were at the tailgate. Slowly, Jani leaned from around the back of the truck. Joe was even farther away now, still trying to catch Freedom.

She and Penny kept low as they crept to the passenger side door. As quietly as she could, Jani pulled the door open. Hailey was lying on the seat, swathed in a mass of blankets.

"Hailey," Jani whispered. She reached out and shook the girl's shoulder. "Hailey, come with us. Hurry!" The small form didn't move.

"Is she okay?" asked Penny, sudden tears in her voice. "Do you think she's…"

"Hailey, wake up," Jani whispered urgently in the girl's ear. "We're here to save you."

Hailey's eyelids flickered and then she opened one eye. "Jani?"

"Yeah. You have to get up, right now," she said, trying to keep the fearful urgency from her voice. "Penny and I will take you home, okay? But we have to hurry before Joe sees us." She looked up. Joe was still after the black filly. Thank goodness for Freedom's uncanny intelligence and bravery! Jani herself would've been terrified to face the man, but the filly seemed able to handle it, keeping mere inches from his reach and steadily, resolutely, leading him away from the truck.

Jani looked down again to see Hailey resting peacefully with eyes closed.

"Hailey, wake up." Penny's voice was a bit too loud. "What's wrong with her, Jani? Do you think Joe hurt her? We have to get her out of here fast. Freedom's not going to distract him for long." Her words were coming faster and faster. "He's going to come back any second. Or he'll turn around. All he has to do is turn around and see us and he'll be on us in seconds. We have to –"

"We have to pack her," said Jani, firmly. She glanced back at Joe. Now he was just standing there, staring at Freedom and muttering. Jani bent over Hailey's ear. "We're going to carry you, okay, Hailey?"

"Okay," the young girl whispered. She tried to push herself in a sitting position, but failed and sank back down.

Penny grabbed one of Hailey's arms and Jani grabbed the other.

"My mom, is she okay?" Hailey's words were so quiet that Jani almost didn't hear her.

"Yeah, she's fine, just very worried about you. Everyone is."

The two girls dragged Hailey to the edge of the seat, then gently lowered her out of the truck. Her blankets fell into the mud as, almost running, they carried her toward the trees. Jani almost tripped over a big rock as they scrambled the last few feet. Keeta nickered softly when they reached her and nuzzled Hailey's hair with a worried expression on her long face.

"Hold onto her while I get on Keeta," said Jani. "Then you can push and I can pull to get her on with me."

Penny nodded. "Be quick."

"Jenny!" It was Joe's voice.

Jani almost dropped Hailey.

"What do we do?" Penny sounded on the verge of meltdown.

Desperately, Jani searched her brain. What could they do? Hide in the woods until he gave up and went home? But Hailey needed medical attention *now*. Make a run for it, all three of them, on the horses? But they couldn't go very fast with Hailey so weak. Neither of them was strong enough to hold the young girl aboard a horse that was moving quickly and Joe would easily catch them.

“Jenny!” He was coming closer. Somehow, Jani pushed the sound of his boots slopping through the mud from her mind. Blocked the sound of his voice. She had to think. She had to be reasonable. He hadn’t seen them yet or he’d be running toward the trees. However, he’d spot them the second they emerged from the dark forest. How were they going to cross the bridge and get away while he was there?

“What do we do?” Penny repeated, her voice a whispered sob. “He’s going to kill us.”

What would Freedom do? Jani thought. *She’s been so cool and reasonable, even when Joe was just inches away from her.*

Suddenly Jani’s mind came clear. There was only one way to get Hailey away. They had to play the same game Freedom had. One of them had to slowly and steadily ride toward civilization with Hailey – after the other led Joe on a wild goose chase. And the decoy rider had to be her. There was no way she could ask Penny to do something so scary or dangerous. Just like Freedom, she too would have to face Joe.

JANI

Moments after Jani told Penny her plan, Sunny was untied and Penny was on his back. She scooted back so she was sitting behind the saddle and held the reins in one hand. "Whoa, boy," she murmured to the gelding, then leaned down and grabbed Hailey's arm. She pulled upward as Jani pushed the young girl from the ground.

Jani was surprised at how light Hailey felt as she helped her into the saddle. She pushed Hailey's leg over to Sunny's far side and, finally, the girl was aboard. When she let her go, Hailey's mouth opened in a groan and she slumped forward over the saddle horn. Penny immediately wrapped her arms around Hailey's waist and pulled her up.

"You can fit in the saddle too," observed Jani.

"She's so skinny," said Penny, shuffling forward. She sounded breathless – just the way Jani felt.

Jani's legs shook as she mounted Keeta.

"Be careful," said Penny.

As one, they looked toward the road. The truck door was still open and Jani could see Joe in the meager light – he'd found the blankets in the mud. And now he was looking toward them.

Fear tingled in her veins. She closed her eyes for a moment and tried to collect her courage. She had to stay just out of reach. But how was she going to get him to follow her? Wouldn't it be obvious there was only one person in the saddle?

If only Freedom could help her with this too, but – she looked wildly about – there was no sign of the filly.

"Good luck," Penny whispered.

Jani felt too sick to answer her. There was no time to search for Freedom. Joe was walking toward them. She touched Keeta's side with her heels and the mare angled toward the road behind the truck, full of nervous energy. Too quickly, they left the safety of the trees. Jani had to think of a plan, and now! She had to give Joe a reason to chase them.

Jani would have smiled when she realized the answer if she hadn't been so worried about Freedom. Joe would chase her if he thought Hailey was on the horse with her. She just needed to stay far away from the truck lights so he couldn't see her clearly and talk to Hailey as if she were aboard the horse.

Keeta's hooves crunched the stones on the gravel road and in the same instant that Joe turned toward the sound, Jani turned Keeta to trot away from him, back the way he'd come. She poked her elbows out to the side to make her slicker billow outward, hoping that would be enough to fool Joe, and looked back.

Joe was racing toward them, his face hard in the lights, and his arms reaching! How could he move so quickly?

Jani's heart leapt into overdrive and she felt speechless, immobile. Then she screamed, "Hold on, Hailey!"

Keeta lunged forward, then settled into an animated trot. She strained against the reins, almost pulling the slippery wet leather through Jani's fingers. "Calm down, Keeta. It's okay," she murmured to the mare, though she didn't blame the horse for being freaked out – Joe looked like an insane madman running after them.

Jani bounced a bit from side to side in the saddle,

hoping to create the illusion of two bodies. Joe might not see because of the darkness, but if his eyesight was good, he might catch a glimpse now and then.

She looked for Freedom as they sped along the old logging road but there was still no sign of her. The sick feeling bloomed in Jani's stomach. Where was she? Did she need help? Had she slid into the river?

A sudden sound right behind them made her look back, relief warming her face. Freedom! But it wasn't Freedom! It was Joe, just inches behind Keeta, running hard, his hands grasping!

Jani screamed. She couldn't help it. Then she leaned over Keeta's neck and the mare surged into a gallop. Joe was left behind in a split second.

"Stop!" he yelled. But Jani had no intention of stopping. Not until she put some distance between herself and the insane hermit who was trying to nab her!

Suddenly, a dark form rushed in front of Keeta. Jani would have screamed again if she could have – her nerves were totally shot – but Keeta stopped so quickly that she was thrown forward onto the mare's neck. As she shimmied back into the saddle, her movements jerky with panic, she recognized the small horse nuzzling Keeta's muzzle. "Freedom."

"Stop!" The sound was coming from farther away.

Jani looked back. Joe was hidden in the night.

He must have stopped when she and Keeta raced away from him and then seen Penny and Hailey trying to escape! She had to get back!

She spun Keeta around and asked the mare to gallop. "Let's go, Freedom," she called, but there was no need. The filly was there beside them now, matching her dam stride for stride with her long thin legs.

She caught sight of Joe ahead of them, running toward the bridge, waving his arms and yelling. The rain, combined with the thunder of Keeta and Freedom's hooves, was too loud to hear what he was shouting, but Jani didn't care about that. She was just glad he was making noise – that way he wouldn't hear her approach him from behind.

Closer, closer. They raced past the truck and Jani heard the pings of gravel hitting the windshield – a few more yards – and they were flying past Joe.

"…she needs to…" Then Joe's words were drowned out by the rain and river and the noise of Keeta and Freedom's hooves on the bridge.

Sunny trotted ahead, still illuminated in the truck's headlights. They were going so slow! But it didn't matter. They'd enter the washout before Joe could chase them in his truck, and he wouldn't be able to go any further than that. They'd won. They'd rescued Hailey! Now they just had to get her to safety as soon as possible.

Jani pulled Keeta to a slow trot as soon as they came alongside Sunny and looked over at Penny's wet, white face. "We did it," she said and smiled triumphantly.

Penny smiled back at her. "We did it."

She stopped Sunny at the washout. "Should I go first?"

"Sure. Just give me a second to put the lead rope on Freedom. The water looks like it's gotten higher." Swiftly, Jani untied the lead rope from the leathers on Keeta's saddle.

"I'm glad you found her. I was so worried," said Penny.

"Actually, she found me."

"Where is she?"

"She's right…" Jani's words froze in her throat. Freedom wasn't there. "She's gone again," she gasped, and then called shrilly, "Freedom! Freedom!" Why was the filly always running off? She just couldn't understand it. Every time Freedom had done something, it had turned out well: she'd helped them discover Hailey, she'd stopped Joe's truck, and she'd stopped Keeta just in time for Jani and Keeta to race back over the bridge before Joe reached it. But this time they needed to get across the washout, and right away.

"Freedom!" Penny yelled, joining Jani, but no dark form materialized from the night.

There was a sudden rumble and both girls jerked their attention back to the bridge and the distant headlights. Joe was coming! They had seconds, mere seconds, before he reached him. They had to start across the washout.

But they couldn't leave Freedom behind!

"You go across," Jani said suddenly, turning to Penny, though she couldn't bear the thought of being left behind at the water's edge when Joe arrived.

"I'm not going to leave you here."

"But we don't have a choice. Hailey needs a doctor. And I can't go, not without Freedom." The words that Jani couldn't say fluttered inside her throat: if she and Keeta went across and Freedom later tried to follow, the small horse would be swept away and probably killed.

Beside her, Penny gasped. "Jani, look," she said and pointed back at Joe's truck. It was on the move, chugging the last few yards to the bridge. But Penny wasn't pointing at the truck. She was pointing at the slight, dark figure galloping back across the bridge, determination and resolve in every stride.

Freedom was stopping Joe again – but this time, it was for nothing. This time she was simply putting them all at risk.

FREEDOM

There was something wrong with man at the truck when he first tried to catch her. He seemed terrified of her, frightened almost out of his wits, and yet he inched toward her again and again. At first, it made Freedom feel oddly satisfied, as if she'd won somehow – Monster Man was more afraid of her than she was of him.

But after a few minutes of their cat and mouse game, she became curious. *Why* was he so afraid of her? Why was he still moving forward, trying to catch her, when he was so obviously afraid? And there were other things that didn't seem to fit with her idea of him. He spoke to her gently and kindly. He didn't try to hurt her by throwing rocks to scare her away. Instead, he simply pleaded with her to let him pass.

When he hurried back to the truck, apparently to check on Hailey, and discovered her gone, fear beyond anything Freedom had yet seen, leapt into his eyes. Fear for the girl. She watched him from the darkness as he made his futile search around the truck, and again she wondered if he really was the monster she'd first thought.

When Jani popped out of the night and the man started to chase her, for a moment Freedom doubted her new impressions – but only until she saw that his speed was fueled by desperation, his movements motivated by alarm for the sick girl that he obviously thought rode before Jani.

The moment Keeta surged into a gallop, the man turned

and caught sight of Penny, Sunny, and Hailey in the distant headlights. As he ran back the way he'd come, painfully aware he had been misled, Freedom leapt into action. Jani and Keeta had to get back across the bridge before the man reached it, and thanks to her intervention, they did.

And that was the end of it.

Or was it?

As Freedom galloped across the bridge beside Keeta, she knew with dreadful certainty that the bridge was close to collapse. Something as heavy as the man's truck could be the catalyst to send it crashing into the river – and yet the man was so worried about Hailey, he might follow them. He cared about this girl. He might even mistakenly believe that Jani and Penny were the aggressors.

This man wasn't her responsibility, she argued. He was Monster Man. He had hurt her in the past, maybe not directly, but certainly indirectly. And what had he done to her Gentle One, his own daughter? There'd been no sign or scent of her at the house where they'd both once lived.

And yet she couldn't erase his tortured eyes from her mind. If he was a monster, how could he feel so strongly for Hailey? Why would he approach Freedom so kindly, even as fear oozed from him like a black fog? Wasn't that something only a naturally compassionate person would do?

Was it feasible that she'd been wrong all these years? Was it possible that he wasn't a monster?

Her gait slowed. Her hooves turned her around, then carried her back. As she swept toward the man and truck rumbling toward her, a wild whinny burst from her mouth. She could not let this man die. She could not! He knew what it was like to care for another, to step forward in the face of fear. And wasn't that enough reason to save him?

JANI

Jani watched in horror as the truck moved toward Freedom – then the brakes squealed. The truck stopped mere inches from the filly.

"Freedom! Come here!" Jani yelled. Freedom looked back at Keeta and Jani racing toward her, then backed a few paces onto the bridge. The truck crept forward.

When the front tires touched the planks, the truck stopped again. Joe opened the door, and once outside, balanced himself by gripping the hood. Amazement lit up his face as he watched the filly.

"Leave her alone!" Jani shrieked as she trotted nearer.

Joe looked up at her, surprised, then shook his head. His mouth moved but Jani couldn't hear the soft words above the river's roar.

She stopped Keeta a few yards back from Freedom and called again, but the filly still wouldn't come. Again, Joe shook his head and said something unintelligible, then he must have realized that Jani couldn't hear him. He held his hands up where she could see them and stepped forward, an innocent look on his face.

And Freedom stepped toward him! Sniffed at his wet jacket.

Jani felt her mouth drop open. What was happening? Freedom was no longer afraid of Joe. Even worse, she seemed to *like* him.

Cautiously, Joe stroked the filly's neck, then looked up

at Jani, motioned to her and himself, then pointed off of the bridge. He wanted to talk to her but only on the road.

Jani tightened her grip on the reins and nodded. The shaking bridge was making her nervous anyway. She directed Keeta toward the truck as Joe backed up before her, giving her lots of space.

Back on the gravel, she turned Keeta to face the bridge. If Joe came too close or rushed at her, she could trust Keeta to gallop away in time. Penny and Sunny were still standing at the distant washout's edge, Hailey like a rag doll in Penny's grip.

Jani looked back to see Joe advancing slowly with Freedom following him. Weird! "Stop there!" she yelled above the river's roar. He stopped. He'd heard her – which meant he was close enough to yell back to her now.

But now he seemed tongue-tied. Though rain streaked down his face, Jani was surprised to see he was crying; the truck lights illuminated red, swollen, and blinking eyes. He rubbed a hand across his nose, then seemed to remember it was rude to wipe your nose on your hand and let it fall to his side. "She saved me," he finally croaked. "After everything I did to her."

"Who saved you?"

He motioned to the filly. "Freedom stopped me from driving onto this bridge. It would've collapsed for sure with the weight of the truck. I could tell as soon as I walked on it. She saved me, even though Jenny wasn't in the car."

Jani's face hardened. "Her name's Hailey."

"I knew she had a name. I just didn't know what it was. And you need to get her to a hospital, and real fast. She's sick."

"I know. We're only still here because Freedom

turned back. Come on, Freedom. Let's go." Jani asked Keeta to walk and the filly quickly followed.

"Wait. You have to let me help you." Joe sounded desperate.

Jani ignored him and kept going.

"It'll take you too long to get help by taking the road, and I know a shortcut."

Jani didn't bother looking back. She couldn't trust Joe and they couldn't wait any longer to get help for Hailey.

"Freedom knows I'm telling the truth. Look at her. She believes me."

Jani pulled Keeta to a halt and turned, dreading what she would see. Her fears were confirmed when she saw the filly had stopped. "Come on, Freedom," she pleaded, but the filly merely glanced at her before turning to walk back to Joe. Emotion filled Jani's throat. Why was her filly acting this way?

"She's not betraying you," Joe said gently, as if he understood how she felt. "She can tell I'm not lying to you, that's all. Plus she can see I'm stronger than you girls. I can hold Hailey in the saddle as we gallop."

"But we can't trust you."

"If Freedom can trust me…" He cleared his throat, "… if she can forgive me for the past…" His voice trailed off and he stuffed his hands in his pockets.

Jani looked at Freedom standing beside the man. She obviously believed Joe and didn't want to leave without him. If they were going to save Hailey, they might *have* to take him with them. She could only pray that Freedom was right in her assessment of his character.

"Okay." She pushed the word through gritted teeth. "But don't even think of running off with her. We know you have her now and we'll ride for the police if you try anything funny."

Joe nodded. "I would do the same," he said and headed across the shaking bridge toward Penny, Sunny, and Hailey.

Now that she'd gotten her way, Freedom frolicked to Keeta's side. Keeta nuzzled her foal affectionately, her soft nicker lost to the river. Jani whipped out the lead rope and clipped it to her halter – Freedom had caused enough trouble for one night – then she, Keeta, and Freedom hurried to pass Joe before Penny panicked and plunged Sunny into the water.

JANI

Penny was adamant that they shouldn't trust Joe. She wasn't convinced until Hailey suddenly lurched in her arms. If Sunny hadn't stepped quickly to the side, Hailey would have tumbled to the ground.

"We have to decide this in a hurry," said Joe, worried eyes on Hailey's white face.

Jani nodded to her friend.

"Okay!" Penny yelled, frustrated and angry. "But you better not hurt her. Or Sunny either. Or I'll… I'll…"

"I won't hurt either of them," said Joe as he stepped forward. He pulled Hailey out of Penny's arms and held her gently. As soon as Penny was out of the saddle, he asked her to hold Sunny's head and in one graceful movement, was aboard the gelding with Hailey still in his arms. He smiled at Penny when she put the reins in his left hand. "Thanks."

Penny didn't bother answering as she hurried to Keeta and climbed up behind Jani.

"Ready?" Joe called back.

"Ready."

Joe directed Sunny down the bank and started splashing through the current. Jani had been right. The water racing through the washout was deeper. She snubbed Freedom's lead rope to the saddle horn. There was no way she was going to let her be carried away by the renegade river. Keeta plunged down the bank, Freedom right beside her. In a matter of seconds, Freedom was at the end of her lead rope, swimming in the high water, the current rushing around her like she was a stone. Wonderful, steady Keeta just kept on, one step after the other, firmly and carefully walking to the other side of the raging torrent.

The mare scrambled up the other side and kept walking, forcefully pulling Freedom from the clutches of the water. The filly scrambled up on the bank, panting and glistening with the wet, but there was no time for rest. Finally, they were able to get help for Hailey, and not a moment too soon. The girl was completely unconscious, her pale face half-hidden in the crook of Joe's arm.

"Follow me," said Joe, and he encouraged Sunny to trot. Soon they were cantering, and then galloping. The road whipped past like a racing treadmill beneath their pounding hooves.

"What's he doing?" Penny yelled in Jani's ear when Joe turned Sunny off the road.

"He knows a shortcut."

"I hope that's true, Jani," Penny said in a quiet voice. Jani did too. If Joe had fooled Freedom and really was a bad guy, he could be leading them someplace even more remote where he could lock them all up so they could never tell anyone about Hailey. No one would ever know where they were, no one would ever come to save them.

Only Hailey's defenselessness stopped her from turning Keeta around and galloping away from Joe. They couldn't desert her. And besides, she'd seen Joe's eyes, full of concern for Hailey, full of apology for Freedom. He *couldn't* be that bad. He *had* to be telling the truth. Right?

She was so busy thinking and directing Keeta so that Freedom could run beside her while staying on the trail, that at first she didn't notice the lights ahead. They were approaching a house through the trees. And it had hardly taken them any time at all!

The three horses thundered across the field at the back of the house, then slid to a halt on the house owner's soggy back lawn. Penny jumped to the ground, Jani right behind her.

"You follow Joe," said Penny above the rain. "I'll take care of these guys."

Jani nodded. Joe was already halfway to the house and one of them certainly needed to watch him in case this was part of a diabolical plan.

"Come inside as soon as you can," she yelled and ran after Joe and poor, sick Hailey.

Joe motioned to the back door, breathing hard. Jani pounded on the door.

"No, just open it. Go inside," he panted.

Jani turned the knob and pushed the door open, then stepped into the dimly lit foyer.

"Silas! Mary! Come here. It's an emergency!" Joe bellowed between breaths.

A light turned on upstairs and seconds later, another elderly man was descending in his pajamas and bathrobe. "What's happening, Joe?"

A woman appeared at the top of the stairs.

"We need an ambulance. This is Hailey, the girl that went missing," said Jani. The woman ran back to her room to make the call.

"Bring her to the living room," said Silas, leading the way. "We'll warm her up while Mary's phoning for the ambulance."

As she followed Joe to the living room, Jani felt only relief. Freedom had been right about the old hermit. He was only concerned with Hailey's well being.

Now all she could do was pray that they'd gotten medical attention for Hailey in time.

JANI

Silas and Mary's living room was soon bright and warm. Mary brought a quilt for Hailey and offered one to Jani, but Jani couldn't rest yet. She asked Mary if they had a barn for the horses and after Mary said yes and told her that their horses were very welcome to stay, Jani hurried outside to help Penny. Soon Sunny, Keeta, and Freedom were enjoying a well-earned rest in the stalls beside Mary's and Silas's big draft horse. The big Shire seemed overjoyed to have company, and was especially intrigued by Freedom. Her eyes followed the foal constantly.

Jani and Penny piled thick straw in the boxes, filled the mangers with sweet smelling hay and the water buckets with cool, clear water. Penny found horse blankets for Keeta and Sunny but since there were no foal-sized blankets available, Jani couldn't put a blanket on Freedom. However, the barn was cozy, and she knew the foal could cuddle up to her warm dam if she felt chilled.

She gave Keeta a kiss on the nose before they left the barn. "You were so brave tonight, Keeta. Thank you so much." Then she reached to stroke the black filly's forehead. Freedom nickered to her. "And you, little miss. How do you know these things? You're amazing." Freedom looked at her with twinkling blue eyes – she was definitely amused at Jani's awe. The rascal!

"She's more than amazing," Penny said, joining them after fastening Sunny's rug. "It's uncanny the things she knows."

Jani just nodded, her heart too full of love for the two horses to speak.

"Let's go. The ambulance should be here soon," said Penny. "I want to make sure Hailey's okay."

The two girls hurried back to the house, but the ambulance hadn't yet arrived. Mary ushered them into the living room where Hailey lay, still and white, on the couch. Silas and Joe sat in overstuffed chairs, looking worried.

"Is she okay?" Jani asked Mary, afraid to hear the answer.

"She's alive, and that in itself is a miracle," Mary said. "One thing we can be sure of, to survive that accident and then be swept away by the river – well, she's a tough girl."

"Tough enough to hang on until help arrives," added Silas.

Joe said nothing.

"She's diabetic," said Jani.

For a moment, raw fear marked Mary's face, but then she neutralized her expression. "You girls are soaked. I don't have any clothes your size in the house, but I do have quilts. My hobby, you see. It'll be nice to see them getting some use." She bustled from the room but was back in a minute, two stunning quilts in her arms.

Jani selected a turquoise, cream, and lilac colored one, and Penny took the green, gold, and russet one.

"Are you sure?" asked Penny. "We'll get them dirty."

"They'll wash," said Mary.

"The ambulance is here," said Silas and jumped up from his chair.

Jani threw the beautiful quilt around her shoulders and hurried to the front door with the others. Silas's hearing was incredible. Jani didn't hear the ambulance siren until he opened the door. Then it came into view, lights flashing and siren wailing. The attendants turned off the siren when they pulled into the driveway. Quickly they backed up to the porch steps.

A man and woman, in white and blue uniforms, jumped out of the ambulance and hurried through the rain to the porch.

"This way," said Mary. Jani felt tears come to her eyes as Mary, like a big, beautiful angel taking everyone under her wing, led them toward the living room where Hailey lay. Silas followed the ambulance attendants, and for the first time, Jani noticed that Joe hadn't come out into the foyer with them.

She hurried to the living room door. There was Mary, helping Joe stand. He'd been kneeling beside Hailey, his eyes wet. "I found her on the riverbank and I was going to bring her into town tomorrow. I had to fix my truck first, you see? And I don't have a telephone," he explained. "But then she started getting sick."

"Was she walking before? Talking?"

"Yes, both. But she didn't know who she was."

The woman attendant knelt over Hailey and her fingers ran lightly over the girl's head, pausing to linger near her right ear. "She's had a blow to the head," she said.

Together, both attendants rolled Hailey gently onto her back, then while the man checked the rest of Hailey's body, the woman took her pulse rate and checked her breathing.

"Nothing seems to be broken," he said.

"Let's get her prepped for transport," said the woman, as she fit an oxygen mask over Hailey's nose and mouth. "I can do the blood glucometer test once we're underway."

"Good plan."

The woman fit a stiff collar around Hailey's neck while the man tied her legs together. Then they bundled her in some blankets and swiftly lifted her to the waiting stretcher.

"How about you girls?" the male attendant asked, as he and the woman carried Hailey toward the door. "Are you two okay?"

"We're fine."

"The police will want a statement about what happened tonight. Leave your names and addresses with Mary and I'll get the police to contact her, and you, tomorrow. We don't have time to collect the information right now."

Jani nodded. There was no way she was going to get away with not telling her parents now. She and Penny watched from the front door as the ambulance attendants loaded Hailey into the back and drove out the driveway. At the main road, they turned on their siren and sped away.

"Come inside, girls," said Mary, her voice kind. "Do you want me to phone your parents? Don't worry about your horses. You can keep them here as long as you need. Duckie will love the company."

"I can phone," said Jani. "And my mom and dad can pick both of us up. Penny can write down our names and stuff for you."

Mary showed Jani the phone in the kitchen, then discreetly left the room.

Jani took a deep breath as she picked up the receiver. How on earth was she going to explain this to her parents? If only the ambulance attendants hadn't asked them to leave their names and addresses. Now she had to tell. If the police came to her house for a statement and her parents knew nothing about their adventures tonight they'd be far more upset than if she told them tonight.

She sighed as she punched in the number.

There was one ring and then a desperate, "Jani! Is that you? Are you okay? Where are you? Is Penny with you?"

"Yeah, it's me," said Jani, relieved she'd decided to call. Her mom obviously already knew she was gone. "And Penny and I are both okay."

"You have a lot of explaining to do when you get home, young lady. Now where are you? We'll be right there."

A minute later, Jani hung up the phone. She cuddled the quilt even tighter around herself and strode back to the living room. She had to hurry if she wanted to get any answers from Joe before her parents arrived. As soon as she entered the room, Mary got up and offered her comfy looking chair to Jani. "I'll go make us all some tea. You three need to warm up."

"Thanks, Mary, for everything."

After Mary left, an expectant silence filled the room. Jani was about to speak, even though Silas was still there, when he seemed to realize they wanted to talk to Joe alone. "I'll go help Mary," he announced and left.

"So tell us what happened," Jani demanded as soon as he was gone.

"All of it," added Penny. "We want to know all of it."

Joe stared at them with bloodshot eyes. He looked like a wreck. "With Hailey, I don't know what happened. She wandered up from the river, looking like a drowned rat, and I took her home."

"She wouldn't go home with a stranger," Jani said, disbelieving.

Joe shook his head. "She didn't remember anything. So I..." He looked down at his hands. "Well, I lied to her. I told her I was her grandfather. But she needed to get warm and dry. I was planning on telling her as soon as I got her to the hospital," he said, looking up again. "But, she found out by herself. She locked herself in Jenny's room. I got her to take a plate of food into the room and then there was this terrible silence. Finally, I thought to look in the window from outside and she was there, curled up on the floor, her food uneaten. She'd been too weak to even get back in bed." He shuddered. "I saw then she was sick, terribly sick, and she was too afraid to say anything. I didn't mean to scare her so badly. You have to believe me."

"So why didn't you tell us you had her when we came to your house today, instead of freaking out and running inside?"

Joe looked down at his hands again. "Well, that was because of Freedom. When I saw her, I panicked. I… I thought she'd come back for revenge."

Jani made an exasperated noise. As if they'd believe he was scared of a foal! Ridiculous!

"I know, you think it's stupid and it makes no sense, but you don't know everything about her," said Joe said. "She attacked and crippled my partner. Why wouldn't she go after me? I helped capture her when she was a mustang."

"We *know* you were Hansen's partner, and you did more than just capture her." Jani paused to glance toward the door just in case Mary and Silas came in. "You helped *kill* her."

"No, I would never have done that. And if I'd known that was how it would end, I never would have told Hansen about her. I thought I was doing something special for my Jenny girl, that's all, and then everything went badly. I tried to save Freedom. I did. But there was nothing I could do."

"So tell us what happened," said Penny.

Jani glanced sharply at her friend. She sounded far too gentle.

"When my daughter was a young teenager, she found Freedom caught in a bog. The mustang was just a foal then, so Jenny was able to pull her out, and after that she always dreamed of being friends with Freedom – but it's hard to be friends with a wild horse. Freedom liked her, but she never let Jenny touch her. So I thought I'd get Freedom for her to own. I partnered up with Hansen and told him about the wild herd, and said in payment I wanted first pick of the captured horses." He sighed and wrapped his own quilt tighter around himself. "To make a long story short, Freedom escaped the first time, and when Hansen went after her and caught her himself, he said that since she got away the time *I* helped with the mustangs, that I couldn't choose her. I got a pretty roan filly for Jenny and hoped it would be enough, but I should have known."

"So what did you do?" There was Penny, sounding kind again. How could she?

"When Freedom refused to be broken, I tried to convince him to turn her loose, but he wouldn't listen. Then Jenny found out Freedom was in Hansen's clutches and tried to help her – but by then the poor horse was too weak, too near death, and well, Hansen caught Jenny in the attempt. He told her that I was the one who got Freedom captured and hurt, not him…" He stopped for a moment, and when he continued, his voice was a rough whisper. "She believed him. That night, after I was asleep, she set her roan horse free, then ran away to her Aunt Milly's house. She refused to come home, refused to speak to me, wouldn't even let me apologize."

For the first time, Jani felt a twinge of pity for Joe.

"So I guess in a way, Freedom has already punished me. I lost my girl." He looked up at Jani with tearful eyes. "But what I don't understand is why she saved me."

"Because she realized you'd suffered enough?" suggested Penny.

Jani inhaled deeply. Should she trust this man with Freedom's story? He had put Hailey in danger by panicking over Freedom – but then he'd also saved her life. If he hadn't found her in the forest, she could be dead by now. "No, that wasn't it," she said, making a quick decision. "It's because she let the past go. She even forgave Hansen."

Quickly, Jani told Joe about finding Freedom in the barn as a wild, trapped ghost. He kept interrupting her with exclamations of wonder as she told the story of how she and Penny had freed the mustang's spirit.

"And when her hatred died, she could leave the barn."

"But not before we had a really cool fire," added Penny.

"And then she came back, as Keeta's foal," Jani finished. "But don't ask me to explain that. I can't."

Joe was obviously speechless. He just sat and stared, shaking his head. The doorbell rang and Jani heard Mary greet her mom and dad.

"We should go," she said quietly to Penny.

The two girls rose to their feet, but Penny paused at the doorway. "What about now? Do you ever see your daughter now?"

Slowly, Joe shook his head. "She went off to university and graduated, got a job as a teacher in the town where her aunt still lives. She got married and has children. I've seen them from a distance, that's all."

"That's so sad," said Penny. "Maybe it would help if you told her that Freedom's alright."

Joe shrugged and stared at his hands, looking more lost

and alone than anyone Jani had ever seen. He'd made some mistakes, practiced some poor judgment, but did he deserve this? To lose his family? To spend the rest of his life alone and isolated from the person he loved most of all?

Jani blinked back sudden tears. Even Freedom didn't think so. She'd forgiven Joe for the role he'd played in her past. She'd even saved his life. "Bring Jenny to visit Freedom," she said. "I bet she'll know how to make things better. You can get my address from Mary."

The old man looked up at her in amazement. New tears spilled down his cheeks, then his eyes became brighter. A half smile touched his face. "Thanks," he croaked. "Thank you so much."

HAILEY

Hailey heard a noise and looked up from her book. Two girls stood in the doorway, one holding a beautiful quilt and the other a brightly wrapped box. "Hey, guys. Come in," she said.

"Thanks," said Jani. "We brought you some stuff." She held the quilt out to Hailey.

"Cool," said Hailey, taking the bright material into her hands.

"We all got one. Mary, the lady who phoned for the ambulance, gave us each one."

"It's gorgeous." Hailey traced the stitched artistic design with a finger.

"How are you feeling?" asked Penny.

"A lot better. Thanks to you guys."

"Do you remember everything that happened?"

"I don't remember you coming to rescue me, but Mom told me about it."

"You remember Joe?"

"Yeah, and how scared I was." Hailey frowned.

"He's not such a bad guy, once you get to know him," said Penny, holding out a wrapped box. "For you."

"Thanks." Hailey took the package eagerly and ripped the paper away. She opened the top off the box. "Oh, I love it!" She reached inside to pull out a gold colored, stuffed horse with white mane and tail. "Thanks," she said as she hugged it to her thin body.

"We thought you might want something to remind you how fun it is to ride horses," said Jani.

"Mom told me about that too. I can't believe I actually *rode* a horse!"

"You did pretty well too," said Penny. "Considering that you were unconscious most of the time. Sunny – he's my horse and the one you rode – he's exactly this color." She reached to fluff the toy palomino's mane.

"Cool. I'm going to name this little guy Sunny Two."

Penny laughed. "Perfect."

"We were thinking, Hailey, there's no reason to be afraid of horses anymore, now that you've ridden one and it turned out alright," said Jani. When Hailey glanced fearfully at Penny, she added, "Don't worry. Penny won't tell anyone. Only the three of us will ever know."

"Yeah. And anytime you start to feel a bit afraid, just think of how you rode Sunny as he carried you safely across raging rivers, along torrential trails, and through um… flowery forests?"

"Formidable forests," said Jani.

Hailey smiled. "I'd ride Sunny again in a second. And Keeta too, I think. But the idea of riding some other horse, well, I don't know."

"We can help you choose a horse at the stables that's gentle and kind if you'd like," offered Jani.

"Really?"

"No prob," said Penny. "And Elaine never needs to know."

"I'm going to tell her anyway. I should have told her right at the beginning," said Hailey. "But Jasmine doesn't need to know. Remember your promise; it's a secret."

"I won't tell another soul," said Jani.

Hailey looked down and twirled a strand of Sunny Two's long white hair around her index finger.

"I won't either," said Penny. "I promise too."

Hailey looked up. "You know, I don't care what Jasmine thinks. Let her know I was scared. And let her watch me get over it."

Jani laughed. "Awesome."

Penny's face lit up with a huge grin. "You totally rock, Hailey!"

FREEDOM

Freedom reluctantly raised her head from the green grass. She was getting old enough to eat the succulent blades, and was completely reveling in the glorious taste. She turned to face the back of Jani's barn. Someone was coming. She could hear voices.

Joe's voice. Freedom snorted and edged closer to her dam. She'd been right to trust him the other night – but why was he here now, when Jani was away?

"They mustn't be home," Joe said, as he came into view. Beside him, a woman walked, silent, her face set like stone.

"I really appreciate you coming, Jenny. I know you didn't have to. I know there's no way I can make up for the past, for what I did to Freedom. I'm not trying to do that. I just wanted to show you this… *important*… thing. You'll be glad you came, I promise."

The woman stared off into the distance as she walked.

"I know it must be hard, coming back here," Joe babbled on, obviously nervous. He wanted to impress this woman. Who was she? Freedom didn't recognize her by sight. She raised her nose into the air and sniffed – the scent of flowers and spices entered her nostrils.

Totally unfamiliar.

But wait. Beneath the heady perfume was another smell. A human smell. A human she recognized immediately – Gentle One!

A neigh burst from Freedom's open mouth and she raced toward the fence, Keeta trotting after her.

The woman stopped short. "Oh my."

The filly neighed again and slid to a stop on the other side of the fence.

"That's… that's not *her*, is it?"

Gently, Joe took the woman's arm and led her forward. "She's come back."

"Freedom?" Gentle One was crying now. "I don't understand." She clutched at her father's arm. "She didn't really die? But she did. I was there. And this is a foal, not a horse, and that was years and years ago."

Freedom neighed again, softer this time. She leaned over the fence, trying to get as close as possible to Gentle One, her friend who had saved her once, long ago. How delicious it was to be with her again. Joy coursed through her veins, encircled her heart.

"I'll explain everything," said Joe. When they reached the fence, he stopped and helped his daughter climb over the rails. Then he told her the story of Freedom's rescue from the barn as a wild spirit.

Freedom sniffed her old friend's hair, her face, her hands, then held still as Gentle One caressed her neck and hugged her. "She never let me touch her before, or at least not after that time in the swamp."

"But she was grateful to you for saving her. She loved you, and does still."

"It was so long ago." Gentle One said, sounding amazed. "But you're right, she does. I can see it in her eyes."

"I love you too, Jenny. I hope and pray everyday that maybe, maybe somehow, you can forgive me?"

Slowly, the woman turned to look at her father.

"Telling Hansen about Freedom was the biggest mistake of my life," he continued.

Gentle One bit her lip, breathed deep, then whispered, "I love you too, Dad. And I've missed you."

"Forgive me?"

"Only if you forgive me."

Moments later, Joe was across the fence and his daughter was in his arms. They were both crying, but Freedom knew they weren't sad. She could feel happiness emanating from them like a wild melody, a joyous hymn. She stepped back to her dam, nuzzled her, then bounced away, trying to get Keeta to share in her exuberance.

How wonderful to see her old friend! How perfect to know she was happy and loved by a father who wasn't a monster. All those years she'd believed a lie, but no more.

She stopped when she heard a distant door closing – the front door of the house. Was Jani home? A minute later, her girl's face looked out the upstairs window, first worried and then relieved when she recognized Joe. She smiled down at Freedom, gave a tiny wave, and settled down to watch.

Gentle One and her father released their hug and turned to watch the horses as Freedom played and Keeta grazed. They talked, cried some more, and even laughed together as they set everything right between them. Freedom didn't approach them again – her life was with Jani now – and Gentle One seemed to understand. She seemed content to just watch the filly as she danced around her dam.

When they decided to go, Joe climbed the fence first. Gentle One smiled at her before climbing out of the pasture, then paused on the other side of the fence and leaned on the top rail. "I'm glad everything turned out

well for you, Freedom," she said. "I'm glad for all of us." Then she turned and walked away.

Freedom meandered back to the fence, her ears pricked forward. Would her friend remember their ritual?

Just before going out of sight around the corner, Gentle One looked back and waved, like all the times when she'd visited Freedom in the wild.

Freedom's first human friend waved to her once more, then she took her father's arm, smiled up into his eyes, and walked away by his side.

Freedom's gaze swept up again to Jani in time to see her girl leave the window seat. She'd be down in a matter of seconds. Freedom shivered with anticipation.

What adventure would they have today?